THIRD EDITION

Listen to Me!

Beginning Listening, Speaking & Pronunciation

BARBARA H. FOLEY

INSTITUTE FOR INTENSIVE ENGLISH
UNION COUNTY COLLEGE, NEW JERSEY

NATIONAL
GEOGRAPHIC
LEARNING

HEINLE
CENGAGE Learning

Australia • Brazil • Japan • Korea • Mexico • Singapore • Spain • United Kingdom • United States

**Listen to Me!: Beginning Listening,
Speaking & Pronunciation, Third Edition**
Barbara H. Foley

Publisher: Sherrise Roehr

Acquisitions Editor: Tom Jeff eries

Assistant Editor: Marissa Petrarca

Director, US Marketing: Jim McDonough

Marketing Manager: Caitlin Driscoll

Content Project Manager: John Sarantakis

Print Buyer: Betsy Donaghey

Composition: Pre-Press PMG

Cover Design: The Creative Source

Library of Congress Control Number: 2008939903

ISBN-13: 978-1-4240-0378-5

ISBN-10: 1-4240-0378-4

National Geographic Learning
20 Channel Center Street
Boston, MA 02210
USA

Cengage Learning is a leading provider of customized learning solutions with office locations around the globe, including Singapore, the United Kingdom, Australia, Mexico, Brazil, and Japan.

Cengage Learning products are represented in Canada by Nelson Education, Ltd.

Visit National Geographic Learning online at **elt.heinle.com**

Visit our corporate website at **www.cengage.com**

Printed in the United States of America
3 4 5 6 7   22 21 20 19 18

ACKNOWLEDGMENTS

In the third edition of *Listen to Me!* I was working from an expanded treasure chest. The original text has been used by thousands of students over the past twenty years. By listening carefully, I have been able to apply student and teacher feedback plus new research in the ESL field to add, delete, and change features of the existing program. With much appreciation to the individuals below, the revised edition of *Listen to Me!* is hopefully up-to-date, effective and enjoyable to use.

Thank you to my colleagues at Union County College. You've always been available to share ideas, test materials, and speak into a tape recorder. Special thanks to Howard Pomann, Dorothy Burak, Marinna Kolaitis, Liz Neblett, Larry Wollman, John McDermott, Litza Georgiou, Andre DeSandies, and June Pomann. I also appreciate the support and assistance of Jim Brown, senior editor.

When writing, an author owes a special debt to researchers and theoreticians in the ESL field. Over the past several years, I have read journal articles and books on listening and pronunciation by countless individuals in the ESL field. Additionally, I was privileged to hear all of them speak at International TESOL conferences: Linda Grant, David Nunan, Patricia Dunkel, Stephen Krashen, Joan Morley, Pat Wilcox Peterson, Jack Richards, and Penny Ur.

Finally, thank you, Bill, for your constant support and confidence in me.

CONTENTS

TO THE TEACHER

English language learners are surrounded by sounds—conversations, announcements, music, television, radio, instructions. For many, listening is their primary source of language input. Our challenge as teachers is to help students make sense of this incoming stream of language. As learners, our students need encouragement, practice, and a familiarity with listening strategies. As individuals, they need confidence in their ability to understand their new language.

Listen to Me! Third Edition develops listening skills for beginner students through high interest narratives and informal conversations. Key features include:

- Real-life topics relevant to students' lives.
- A variety of listening comprehension and listening discrimination exercises to foster better listening strategies.
- Integrated pronunciation and grammar exercises to improve and refine students speaking skills.
- Group speaking activities that personalize the language and allow students to use the skills they have learned.

The text and accompanying audio program may be used with college-level students, adult programs, and high school classes. Additionally, the materials are both easy to use and highly effective in a language laboratory.

Listen to Me! is the first of two titles designed to develop aural/oral communication skills. *Now Hear This!* meets the needs of students at the high-beginning to low-intermediate level.

NEW TO THE THIRD EDITION

Teachers who are familiar with the second edition of *Listen To Me!* will be familiar with the thematic, easy-to-use format of the text. But, a look at the table of contents will reveal that the text has been thoroughly updated.

- NEW! Five new units on topics such as The Shopping Mall, The Airport and Alaska make learning more interesting and relevant.
- NEW! Short dictation exercises help students focus on individual sounds, words, and grammar points.
- NEW! More examples of natural speech in the listenings expose students to everyday, real spoken English.
- NEW! Listening Note and Pronunciation Note boxes highlight the listening skills being taught, helping students maximize their learning.
- NEW! Audio CDs with tracking information included next to each appropriate exercise allow students and instructors to easily find the right audio track.

UNIT ORGANIZATION

There are fifteen units in *Listen to Me! Third Edition*. Each is based on an engaging narrative or conversation related to a job, interests, daily activities, or problems. Each unit follows a similar format.

Before You Listen

"Before You Listen" introduces the topic of the unit. The discussion questions in this section stimulate students' interest in the selection and ask for students' experiences and background knowledge. Other activities may ask students to identify states, match occupations, make predictions, look at maps, or discuss photographs. The class also looks at key words for the unit and can ask about any new words they do not understand. The teacher can say the vocabulary words and ask students to repeat them. Then, students complete sentences with the new vocabulary words.

Listening 1: Narrative or Conversation

Students listen to a one-to-three minute Narrative or Conversation. The audio is supported through the use of visuals. The unit includes an illustration that clearly depicts the story, either as one picture or as a series of small sketches. Encourage students to carefully look at the picture, noting actions, relationships, and sequence of events. A specific listening strategy is also explained, directing students to attend to features such as using visuals, predicting, making guesses, getting the main idea, understanding the relationship between speakers, etc. Students then listen to the recorded story. Most classes will request that the track be played again, one or more times. For some classes, it may be helpful to play the track in sections, a few sentences at a time. After listening, students tell the class any information they remember about the story. The focus here is not on structure, but on the comprehension of the story. One student may only be able to give back one small piece of information. Another may be able to remember many facts. The teacher should prompt students to recall much of the information, especially those parts that are pictured. Students who may have had difficulty understanding the selection will learn from their classmates. As the audio is played additional times, students will be able to pick up more and more of the narrative.

A variety of comprehension activities follow the audio. Students may be asked to identify specific story pictures or to answer questions with a correct number or amount from the story and pictures. Depending on the story, students are asked for specific information. They may identify the jobs of the characters, check the items a person bought in a store, choose the doctor's orders, etc. After some selections, students hear questions about the story and circle the correct answer. The final exercise in this section is entitled *What Do You Think?* Students are asked to express their own opinions about the story and the characters.

Structure and Pronunciation

In the next section, the emphasis shifts to listening discrimination. In the first exercise, students focus on verb tense. Although there is a variety of tenses within each selection, one tense usually predominates. Students complete sentences from the listening passage with the verb in the target tense. This is followed by a short dictation in which students listen to and write five sentences from the listening.

Within each listening selection, there is often a recurring pronunciation feature. The pronunciation exercises help students to focus on word endings, reductions, elisions, intonation, and stress. Students circle the phonological item they hear, complete sentences with the correct word, or mark stress or intonation. The pronunciation exercise often asks the students to sit with a partner and try to repeat the words or sentences with a partner.

Listening 2: Conversations

This section begins with three to six short conversations, interview comments, or announcements related to the topic. The interviews and announcements are transcriptions of authentic language. The conversations are purposely pitched at a more difficult level than the narratives, so that students begin to realize that they do not need to understand every word in a conversation. In the first exercise, students guess the general meaning of the conversation by circling a picture identified in the listening passage. Often, simply by recognizing a few of the vocabulary words or phrases in the exchange, students will be able to make their selections. Further exercises develop listening strategies, helping students to become familiar with common conversation techniques, such as continuing the conversation, checking or repeating information, expressing agreement, disagreement, surprise, etc.

Speaking

The Speaking section offers two or three follow-up speaking activities that allow students to share personal stories, ideas and opinions. In many units, support is provided for students to write and perform short conversations. For the other activities, students sit with a partner or in small groups. The groups should consist of three to four students so that every student has an opportunity to participate.

Audio Script and Index

This section includes a complete audio script for the *Listen to Me!* audio program. Teachers and students can refer to the Index to locate listening strategies, pronunciation points, and key words taught in the text.

BACK IN SCHOOL

BEFORE YOU LISTEN

A Discuss   Talk about these questions.

1. Is speaking English easy for you?

2. How is your English . . . good? so-so? not too good?

3. Where do you speak English?

B Read and Choose   Why are you studying English? Read these statements. Check the reasons that you are in school.

1. ___ I want to find a job.

2. ___ I want to find a better job.

3. ___ I want to understand the radio and television.

4. ___ I want to talk to my neighbors.

5. ___ I want to go to the store and use English.

6. ___ I want to talk to my children's teachers.

7. ___ I want to go to college/ get more education.

C Key Words   Talk about the new words. Then, complete the sentences.

nervous	cafeteria	homework
each other	break	second

1. Our coffee _____ is 15 minutes.

2. I feel _____ when I speak English.

3. I came to the United States last year. This is my _____ year in this country.

4. For _____, we have to do pages 14 and 15.

5. We talk to _____ before class.

6. I'm going to the _____ for a cup of coffee.

LISTENING 1: STORY

Listening Note

You are going to listen to a student talk about her class. Relax and look at the picture. Don't worry if you don't understand some words. You will hear the audio several times. Each time you listen, you will understand more.

CD 1; Track 1

A First Listening Ana is a student at the Dallas Adult School. Look at the picture on page 2 and listen to her story. After you listen, tell the class any information you remember about the story.

CD 1; Track 1

B Listen for Numbers Read these questions about the story. Then listen to the story again and answer these questions with the correct number.

1. What's the date? _____
2. What is the room number? _____
3. How old is Ana? _____
4. How many children does she have? _____
5. How many students are in her class? _____
6. How many are from Mexico? _____
7. How many are from Vietnam? _____
8. How many are from India? _____
9. How old is the teacher? _____
10. How many hours is the class? _____
11. What time does this class begin? _____
12. What time is the break? _____

CD 1; Track 2

C True or False Listen to these statements. Circle *T* if the statement is true or *F* if the statement is false.

1. T F   4. T F   7. T F
2. T F   5. T F   8. T F
3. T F   6. T F   9. T F

D What do you think? Discuss the question with your class.

1. What are the reasons that Ana is back in school?

STRUCTURE AND PRONUNCIATION

CD 1; Track 3

Ⓐ Singular or Plural   Listen and circle the word you hear. Is the word singular or plural?

1. class   classes
2. room   rooms
3. word   words
4. friend   friends
5. teacher   teachers

6. school   schools
7. student   students
8. hour   hours
9. day   days
10. week   weeks

CD 1; Track 4

Ⓑ Dictation   Listen and write the words you hear.

1. _____
2. _____
3. _____
4. _____
5. _____

6. _____
7. _____
8. _____
9. _____
10. _____

Ⓒ Partner Practice   Sit with a partner. Say one of the words in each pair. Your partner will point to the word that you say. Then, change partners and repeat the exercise.

> **Pronunciation Note**
>
> Add *s* to make a noun plural. When you add *s* to a noun, do not add a syllable.
>
> boy-boys   car-cars   teacher-teachers
>
> If a noun ends in *s*, *ss*, *x*, or *z*, add *es* to make the plural. This adds a syllable.
>
> class-classes   house-houses   box-boxes

1. school   schools
2. book   books
3. car   cars
4. student   students
5. house   houses
6. name   names

7. computer   computers
8. country   countries
9. day   days
10. class   classes
11. word   words
12. bus   buses

LISTENING 2: ANNOUNCEMENTS

CD 1; Track 5

Ⓐ Match Ms. Lang, the teacher, made several announcements the first week of school. Write the number of each announcement next to the correct topic.

> **Listening Note**
> When you listen, first try to understand what the conversation or announcement is about. This is called the main idea. Then, try to get more of the details.

Announcement 1   _____ parking sticker

Announcement 2   _____ children

Announcement 3   _____ break time

Announcement 4   _____ other classes

Announcement 5   _____ days absent

Announcement 6   _**1**_ book

Ⓑ Getting the details Listen to each announcement again. Write only one or two words to help you remember the information. Then, sit with a partner and share your information.

CD 1; Track 5

1. Book: _____**$20, main office**_____

2. Break: _____

3. Parking sticker: _____

4. Children: _____

5. Other classes: _____

6. Days absent: _____

Ⓒ Listen and Complete The students are asking Ms. Lang to repeat some information. Listen and complete these conversations.

CD 1; Track 6

1. STUDENT: Excuse me. _____**Where**_____?

2. STUDENT: Excuse me. _____?

3. STUDENT: Excuse me. _____?

4. STUDENT: Excuse me. _____?

5. STUDENT: Excuse me. ____How long is the____?

6. STUDENT: Excuse me. _____can____?

SPEAKING

A Introductions   Listen to the students introduce themselves. What expressions do they use?

1.    2.

B Interaction   Sit in a group of four students. Introduce yourself and spell your name slowly. The other students will write the names of the students in the group.

Students in my group:

1. _____

2. _____

3. _____

C Complete and Practice   Complete the sentences with your group. Practice saying the information.

1. Today is _____ [date].

2. The name of our school is _____.

3. We are in room _____.

4. Our classroom is on the _____ floor.

5. Our teacher's name is _____.

6. The name of our book is _____.

7. There are _____ students in our class.

8. There are _____ men and _____ women.

9. The students are from _____.

10. We have class _____ days a week.

11. Our class starts at _____. It ends at _____.

12. We (have/don't have) a break.

ALI

BEFORE YOU LISTEN

A **Discuss**   Talk about the questions.

1. Do you live in a house or in an apartment?
2. Do you know your neighbors?
3. Are you friendly with your neighbors?
4. What countries are they from?

B **Match**   Match these jobs with the correct picture.

1. _____ x-ray technician
2. _____ mail carrier
3. _____ student
4. _____ school bus driver
5. _____ teacher

C **Key Words**   Talk about the new words. Then, complete the sentences.

aunt	uncle	retired	relatives
single	couple	twins	

1. My sister and I are both 24. We're _____twins_____.
2. I have a lot of _____ in the United States.
3. My father's sister is my _____aunt_____. Her husband is my _____uncle_____.
4. Tom is _____single_____. He isn't married.
5. My father _____retired_____ when he was 65 years old.
6. The married _____ who lives in our apartment building is very friendly.

LISTENING 1: STORY

Listening Note
Looking at a picture or photo as you listen can help you understand what a speaker is saying.

CD 1; Track 8

A First Listening   Read the names below. As you listen to this story, write the names of each person who lives in the apartment building on the picture. Then, tell the class any information you remember about each person.

Ali	Mr. and Mrs. Ramirez	Dahn
Mr. Patel	Manuel and Michael	Kim

CD 1; Track 8

B Match   Read the jobs below. Then listen to the story again. Match each person with his or her job. Answers may be used more than once.

1. _____ Ali   a. a school bus driver

2. _____ Mr. Ramirez   b. a student

3. _____ Mrs. Ramirez   c. an x-ray technician

4. _____ Mr. Patel   d. a mail carrier

5. _____ Dahn   e. a retired teacher

6. _____ Kim

CD 1; Track 9

C Listen for Numbers   Look at the picture. Listen and answer the questions with the correct number.

1. _____   3. _____   5. _____   7. _____

2. _____   4. _____   6. _____   8. _____

CD 1; Track 10

D Comprehension Questions   Listen and circle the correct answer.

1. a. Egypt
   b. Oakdale
   c. his aunt and uncle

2. a. in Egypt
   b. at the university
   c. his aunt and uncle

3. a. on the 1st floor
   b. on the 2nd floor
   c. on the 3rd floor

4. a. Yes, he is.
   b. He's a mail carrier.
   c. He's a school bus driver.

5. a. Egypt
   b. India
   c. next to Ali

6. a. He's retired.
   b. Yes, he is.
   c. No, he isn't.

7. a. Yes, they are.
   b. No, they aren't.
   c. at the university.

8. a. Mr. Patel is.
   b. Ali is.
   c. Mr. Ramirez is.

STRUCTURE AND PRONUNCIATION

Ⓐ Complete   Complete the sentences with *am, is,* or *are.*

1. I _____ a student at Oakdale University.

2. There _____ four families in this building.

3. Mr. Ramirez _____ a mail carrier.

4. Manuel and Michael _____ twins. They _____ ten years old.

5. Mr. Patel _____ old. He _____ a retired teacher.

6. Dahn _____ a student at Oakdale University.

7. All the people _____ friendly.

8. They _____ good neighbors.

CD 1; Track 11

Ⓑ Dictation   Listen and write the sentences you hear.

1. _____

2. _____

3. _____

4. _____

5. _____

6. _____

CD 1; Track 12

Ⓒ Pronunciation   Repeat the expressions that people use to say *Hello* and *Good-bye.*

Hello.	How are you?	Good-bye.
Hello.	How's everything?	Good-bye.
Hi.	How are you?	So long.
Good morning.	Good, thanks.	Take care.
Good afternoon.	Great.	See you later.
Good evening.	Fine.	Have a good day.
		You, too.

What other expressions do you sometimes hear?

LISTENING 2: CONVERSATIONS

A Match   Listen to the conversations and number the pictures.

a. _____   b. _____   c. _____

B Listen and Answer   Listen to each conversation again. Then answer the questions with your class.

1. Who is talking? Why doesn't she use Mr. Patel's first name?

   Who is Mr. Patel waiting for?

   Why is Mrs. Ramirez driving the boys to school?

2. Who is talking?

   Why does Carlos say, "It's going to be a long day."?

3. Who is talking? Why is Ali studying?

   Why does the teacher say, "Good luck."?

C Listen and Choose   Listen and choose the correct response.

1. a. Good.
   b. Good evening.

2. a. Fine, thanks.
   b. Have a good weekend.

3. a. Good-bye.
   b. Hello.

4. a. You, too.
   b. Good morning.

5. a. See you later.
   b. Hi.

6. a. Good afternoon.
   b. I'm fine, thanks.

7. a. How are you?
   b. You, too. Have a good day.

8. a. Great.
   b. See you later.

SPEAKING

A Partner Practice   Sit with a partner and complete the conversation. Then, practice saying the conversation.

B Write a Dialogue   Write a short dialogue with another student, saying hello and good-bye. Act out your dialogue in front of the class.

C Write and Share   Write the name of one person who lives in your apartment building or in your neighborhood. Write three sentences about the person. Share the information with a partner.

Mr. / Mrs. / Ms. _____ lives _____.

1. _____

2. _____

3. _____

CITY OR COUNTRY

BEFORE YOU LISTEN

A Discuss   Talk about the questions.

1. What area do you live in: the city, the suburbs, or the country?

2. Are there many hospitals in your area? What is the name of the nearest hospital? What kind of hospital is it?

B Word Association   What words from the box do you associate with a city? What words do you associate with the country?

> **CITY OR COUNTRY?**
> - museums
> - theaters
> - mountains
> - rivers
> - restaurants
> - lakes

C Key Words   Talk about the new words. Then, complete the sentences.

takes care of	choose	offers	patients	cancer

1. I don't smoke because I don't want to get _____.

2. When a child is sick, a parent _____ him.

3. Can you help me _____ a good doctor?

4. When my sister graduated from nursing school, she received three job _____.

5. A 300-bed hospital has room for 300 _____.

LISTENING 1: STORY

CD 1; Track 15

A **First Listening**   Gloria is going to graduate from nursing school next month. She has two job offers and is trying to decide which job to take. Look at the pictures and listen to the story. After you listen, tell the class any information you remember about the story.

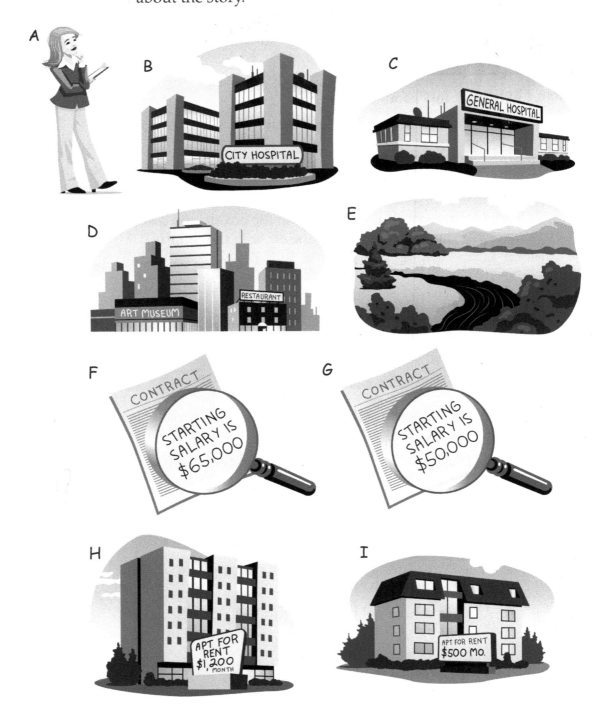

Listening Note

When a speaker is talking about two people, places, or ideas, take a few notes to compare them. Your notes will help you see what is the same and what is different.

B Note-Taking   As you listen to the story again, take a few notes about each job. Keep the same kind of information next to each other.

CD 1; Track 15

City	Country
Large - 600 bed	Small - 50 bed
Cancer hospital	
Salary -	
Rent -	

C Listen and Write the Letter   Listen to the sentences. Write the letter of the correct picture.

CD 1; Track 16

1. ____   3. ____   5. __D__   7. ____   9. __A__

2. ____   4. ____   6. ____   8 __B__

D Comprehension Questions   Listen and circle the correct answer.

CD 1; Track 17

1. a. a student   b. a nurse

2. a. It's large.   b. In the city.

3. a. a large hospital   b. a general hospital

4. a. $50,000 a year   b. $65,000 a year

5. a. the one in the city b. She doesn't know yet.

E What do you think?   Discuss the questions with your class.

1. Which job should Gloria take? Why?

2. Where would you like to live: the city or the country?

STRUCTURE AND PRONUNCIATION

A Complete   Complete the sentences with *is* or *are*.

1. Gloria _____ a student in nursing school.

2. The hospital in the city _____ a cancer hospital.

3. There _____ many restaurants in the city.

4. The other hospital _____ in the country.

5. There _____ 50 beds in the hospital.

6. The salary _____ average.

7. Both job offers _____ good.

B Dictation   Listen and copy the sentences you hear.

CD 1; Track 18

1. _____

2. _____

3. _____

4. _____

5. _____

C Syllables   The first time you listen, write the number of syllables in each word. The second time you listen, mark the stressed syllable. The stressed syllable is longer and louder than the other syllables.

CD 1; Track 19

1. hóspital **3**	7. excellent _____	13. museum _____
2. school _____	8. area _____	14. city _____
3. apartment _____	9. cancer _____	15. country _____
4. mountains _____	10. patient _____	16. offer _____
5. student _____	11. job _____	17. nursing _____
6. care _____	12. salary _____	18. restaurant _____

D Listen for Stress   Listen and repeat the sentences. Put stress on the correct syllable.

CD 1; Track 20

1. Gloria is a student in nursing school.

2. She has two job offers.

3. One hospital is in the city.

4. It's near restaurants, theaters, and museums.

5. It's a cancer hospital.

6. It gives excellent care to its patients.

LISTENING 2: CONVERSATIONS

(A) Listen and Compare   Gloria is talking to her father about the two job offers. He is writing down the information to help Gloria compare the jobs. Listen to the conversations and complete the chart.

CD 1; Track 21

	City Hospital	General Hospital
Salary	$65,000	$50,000
Rent		
Transportation		
Hours (shift)		
Vacation		
Job		

(B) Answer   Look at the information in your chart and answer the questions.

1. In which hospital is the salary higher?

2. Which area has higher rents?

3. In which area is transportation more expensive?

4. What shift does Gloria want to work? Which hospital needs nurses at that time?

5. Which hospital gives more vacation days?

6. In your opinion, which job is more interesting?

(C) Share Your Opinion   Which job would you take? Circle your choice. Then, write three reasons for your decision. Share your reasons with the class.

I would take the job at **City Hospital / General Hospital**.

1. _____

2. _____

3. _____

UNIT 3 **City or Country**   **17**

SPEAKING

CD 1; Track 22

A Interview   Listen to each speaker. What is important in a job to each person?

Interview Question: What's important to you in a job?

1. _____   2. _____   3. _____   4. _____

B Interaction   Sit in a small group. When you are looking for a job, what is important to you? Rank these five items from 1 to 5, then, compare your ideas.

☐   Cost of rent in the area

☐   Transportation to work

☐   Work hours

☐   Medical benefits

☐   Salary

C Discuss   Sit in a group and talk about your jobs.

1. Where do you work? What do you do?

2. Is your job interesting?

3. What hours do you work?

4. How far do you live from your job? How do you get to work?

5. What benefits do you get? Do you have medical benefits?

6. How many vacation days do you have?

7. Do you like your job? Why or why not?

▶ Note: In the United States, it is not polite to ask a person about his or her salary.

THE SHOPPING MALL

BEFORE YOU LISTEN

(A) Discuss   Talk about the questions.

1. What is a mall?

2. What mall is near you?

3. About how many stores are there? Can you name some of them?

4. How often do you shop there?

(B) List   Name two things you can buy in each kind of store.

Clothes store	_____	_____
Sports store	_____	_____
Pet store	_____	_____
Electronics store	_____	_____
Drugstore	_____	_____
Jewelry store	_____	_____
Furniture store	_____	_____

(C) Key Words   Talk about the new words. Then, complete the sentences.

thief	lose	puppy - puppies
steal - stole	reach	probably

1. Our dog had eight _____ last month. Would you like one?

2. Last night a _____ got into our house.
   He _____ $500.

3. I can never _____ my sister on the phone. She's always talking to her friends.

4. I love to shop. I'm _____ going to the mall this weekend.

5. I often _____ my car keys. I can't remember where I put them!

LISTENING 1: STORY

Ⓐ Before You Listen   Look at each person. What is he/she doing?

Listening Note

There are many ways to figure out who a speaker is. Is the voice male or female, old or young? What is the tone of voice, i.e. is the person angry, upset, friendly, speaking to a child? Do you hear an address, such as *Mommy, honey,* or *Ma'am?*

Ⓑ Listen and Write the Number   Listen to each shopper. Write the number of the correct picture. Listen again and explain how you decided who was speaking.

CD 1; Track 23

a. _____   c. _____   e. _____

b. _____   d. _____   f. _____

Ⓒ Listen for Information   Listen to the security manager at the mall talk about the shoppers at the mall. What new information do you hear about each person?

CD 1; Track 24

Ⓓ Match   Listen and write the number of the correct picture.

CD 1; Track 25

1. _____   3. _____   5. _____

2. _____   4. _____   6. _____

Ⓔ Comprehension Questions   Listen and circle the letter of the correct answer.

CD 1; Track 26

1. a. at the mall
   b. at the jewelry store
   c. at the police station

2. a. a watch
   b. sunglasses
   c. a telephone

3. a. at the pet store
   b. at the shoe store
   c. at the ice cream store

4. a. a puppy
   b. an ice cream cone
   c. a baseball

5. a. They're cheap.
   b. They're expensive.
   c. No, they aren't.

6. a. three
   b. four
   c. five

7. a. one
   b. two
   c. three

8. a. soccer
   b. basketball
   c. baseball

Ⓕ What Do You Think?   Read the questions below and discuss your answers.

1. What should the guard do about the thief in the jewelry store?

2. When do stores have big sales?

3. Why does this man enjoy his job? Would you like this job?

STRUCTURE AND PRONUNCIATION

A Present Continuous Tense   Complete these statements with a verb from the box. Use the present continuous tense.

cry   walk
tell   talk
wear   look
steal ask
carry

1. The security guard _____ on the phone.

2. The man _____ a watch.

3. He _____ out of the store.

4. The child in front of the pet store _____.

5. She _____ her mother for a puppy.

6. The couple _____ at cell phones.

7. The clerk _____ them about family telephone plans.

8. The little boy _____ a baseball hat.

9. His father _____ a bag with a baseball bat.

B Dictation   Listen and write the sentences you hear.

CD 1; Track 27

1. _____

2. _____

3. _____

4. _____

5. _____

C Contractions   Listen and repeat the contractions. Then, sit with a partner and practice saying the sentences.

CD 1; Track 28

1. He's putting a watch in his pocket.

2. He's walking out the door with the watch.

3. She's crying.

4. She's trying on sunglasses.

5. I'm always losing my sunglasses.

6. She's buying four pairs of shoes.

7. She's giving her credit card to the clerk.

8. He's wearing a baseball hat.

LISTENING 2: CONVERSATIONS

CD 1; Track 29

A Prices   Listen and write the prices you hear.

$ .49   or   49¢   forty-nine cents

$ 1.25   a dollar twenty-five

$ 37.00   thirty-seven dollars

$ 37.99   thirty-seven dollars and ninety-nine cents

a. _____**50¢**_____   f. _____

b. _____**79¢**_____   g. _____

c. _____   h. _____

d. _____   i. _____

e. _____   j. _____

CD 1; Track 30

B How Much Is It?   Listen to each conversation and write the price.

a. _____   b. _____

c. _____   d. _____

e. _____   f. _____

SPEAKING

A Discuss   Sit in a small group and discuss the questions.

1. What malls are in your area? Which one is your favorite?
2. What are some of the stores in the mall?
3. Is this mall an expensive place to shop?
4. When is the last time you went to the mall?
5. What did you buy?
6. Do you usually use cash or a credit card?
7. Do you shop alone or with a friend or family member?

B Write and Discuss   Name two chain stores where you can buy each kind of item. Which store do you like better? Explain your reasons.

Clothes	_____	_____
Shoe store	_____	_____
Electronics store	_____	_____
Drugstore	_____	_____
Office supplies	_____	_____

C Comparing Prices   Sit alone and write the price of each item. Then, sit in a group and compare your prices and the places you buy each item.

1. a cup of coffee _____
2. a gallon/liter of gas _____
3. a movie ticket _____
4. a CD _____
5. a movie rental _____
6. a notebook _____
7. a pen _____
8. a pair of jeans _____
9. a man's haircut _____
10. a manicure _____

D Write a Conversation   Sit with a partner. Decide on a price for each item. Then, choose one of the items and write a conversation between a sales person and a customer.

$ _____ $ _____ $ _____

THE BUS RIDE

BEFORE YOU LISTEN

Ⓐ Discuss   Talk about the questions.

1. How far do you live from school?

2. How do you get to school?

3. How long does it take you?

Ⓑ On The Bus   Many people take the bus to work or to school. What do people do when they are on the bus?

1. __They read the newspaper._____

2. _____

3. _____

4. _____

Ⓒ Point   Look at the picture on page 26 and point to the following words or items.

exact change	headphones	cane
No Smoking sign	pole	seeing-eye dog

Ⓓ Key Words   Talk about the new words. Then, complete the sentences.

blind	offered
crowded	seeing-eye dog
angry	loud

1. The bus was so __crowded__ that I couldn't find a seat.

2. A _____ person is not able to see.

3. A _____ can help a blind person cross the street safely.

4. Please turn that music down. It's too _____ .

5. A young boy _____ a woman his seat.

6. My boss gets _____ when I'm late for work.

LISTENING 1: STORY

Listening Note
Before you listen, try to guess, or predict, some of the information you are going to hear.

(A) Predict   Debbie is taking the bus today. Before you listen, look at the picture and predict some of the information you are going to hear.

CD 2; Track 1

(B) First Listening   Listen to the story. As you listen, write the name of each person on the picture of the bus. Then, tell the class any information you remember.

Debbie	Michael	Diego	Gina
Mrs. Wu	Charlie	Kevin	

CD 2; Track 2

(C) Who Questions   Answer the *Who* questions about the story. Write the name of the correct person.

1. _____   4. _____
2. _____   5. _____
3. _____   6. _____

CD 2; Track 3

(D) Comprehension Questions   Listen and circle the correct answer.

1. a. She always takes the bus.
   b. Her car is at the service center.
   c. She's late.

2. a. $ .25
   b. $1.50
   c. $2.00

3. a. Yes, she is.
   b. She's going to sit.
   c. She's going to stand.

4. a. She's thinking about her car.
   b. She's thinking about her boss.
   c. She's thinking about her fare.

5. a. He is late for work.
   b. He doesn't have enough money.
   c. He doesn't have exact change.

6. a. His dog is with him.
   b. He's going to work.
   c. He wants to get off at the right stop.

7. a. She's going to ask a friend for a ride.
   b. She's going to drive.
   c. She's going to take the bus.

STRUCTURE AND PRONUNCIATION

A Present Continuous Tense   Choose the correct verb from the box and complete the sentences in the present continuous tense.

take	move
listen	stand
get	look
steal	

1. Debbie ___**is getting**___ on the bus.

2. The bus is crowded, so some people _____.

3. This morning many people _____ the bus to work.

4. Mrs. Wu _____ for a seat.

5. One boy _____ to his radio.

6. The bus _____ very slowly.

7. A woman _____ a man's wallet.

B Dictation   Listen and write the sentences you hear.

CD 2; Track 4

1. _____

2. _____

3. _____

4. _____

5. _____

C His, Her, Him   Listen and complete the sentences with *his*, *her*, or *him*. Listen again and repeat the sentences. Then, sit with a partner and practice saying the sentences.

CD 2; Track 5

Pronunciation Note

In spoken English, the *h* in *his, her,* and *him* is usually silent.

1. Debbie is thinking about _____ boss.

2. She's using _____ cane.

3. He's offering _____ seat to Mrs. Wu.

4. She's stealing _____ wallet.

5. Kevin is on the bus with ___*his*___ seeing-eye dog.

6. Jet gets _____ to and from work.

7. He can't hear _____.

8. She's going to ask _____ friend for a ride.

LISTENING 2: CONVERSATIONS

 A Match   Listen to these conversations between people on the bus. Number each picture.

CD 2; Track 6

____   ____   ____

____   ____   ____

 Listening Note
People often check information they hear to be sure that they have the correct time, date, place, and other facts. They repeat the information using question intonation.

 B Listen for Information   Listen to each conversation. Complete with the correct place and time.

CD 2; Track 7

1. At the _____**library**_____ at ____**4:00**____?

2. In the _____ at _____?

3. At the _____ at _____?

4. By the _____ at _____?

5. In _____ at _____?

6. At your _____ at _____?

7. On the _____ at _____?

SPEAKING

Ⓐ Discuss   Sit in a group of three or four students. Talk about the questions.

1. Where do you live? How far is that from school?

2. How do you get to school?

3. How long does it take you to get to school?

4. Do you ever get a ride or give someone a ride?

5. Is the traffic in your area heavy in the morning?

6. Does your school have parking for students?

7. Do you ever take public transportation?

8. Is the bus stop or station near your house?

9. How much is the fare? Do you need exact change?

CD 2; Track 8

Ⓑ Listen for Information   Listen to each speaker talk about getting to school. Complete the information and write one sentence about each person.

1. She _____**takes the bus.**_____.

   It takes her about __**40**__ minutes.

   _____**She takes a city bus.**_____

3. She _____.

   It takes her about _____ minutes.

   _____

2. He _____.

   It takes him about _____ minutes.

   _____

4. He _____.

   It takes him about _____ minutes.

   _____

Ⓒ Interview   Interview another student in your group. Write three sentences about how the student gets to school.

THE AIRPORT

BEFORE YOU LISTEN

Ⓐ Discuss   Talk about the questions.

1. What airport is near your school?

2. How often do you fly?

3. How often do you go to the airport to pick up friends or family?

4. Do you know anyone who works at the airport? What do they do?

Ⓑ Write the Action   Write the action under the correct location in an airport.

sit and wait	take off	empty your pockets
take off your shoes	board the plane	land

Security Line	Gate	Runway
take off your shoes	_____	_____
_____	_____	_____

Ⓒ Key Words   Discuss the new words. Then, complete the sentences.

take off	cancelled	delayed
still	upset	flight

1. _____ 672 from Seattle to San Diego is now boarding.

2. The flight did not _____ on time.

3. The flight was _____ two hours because of heavy rain.

4. Because of the snow, the airlines _____ all flights.

5. I got to the airport at 1:00. It's 6:00 and I'm _____ here!

6. My boss was _____ when her flight was cancelled. She had an important meeting in Boston.

LISTENING 1: TELEPHONE CALLS

Listening Note

When you hear a telephone conversation, you only hear one of the speakers. You can often understand the relationship between the speakers, the location of the speakers, and what they are talking about.

CD 2; Track 9

A First Listening   It's raining hard and all flights at this airport are delayed or cancelled. Look at the picture and listen to each person's telephone call. Point to the person who is talking.

CD 2; Track 9

B Listen and Complete   Listen again. Where is each person? Who is he/she speaking to? The possible locations are: *at the gate, on the security line, at the car rental counter, on the plane, at a restaurant.*

Speaker	Location	Person
1. Samip		
2. Sarah		
3. Jack		
4. Gloria		
5. Carly		

C Identify the Speaker   Write the name of the correct speaker.

1. _____ is sitting on a plane.

2. _____ is on a business trip.

3. _____ is coming home from seeing her father.

4. _____ isn't going to stay at the airport.

5. _____ is going to visit his grandchildren.

D What do you think?   Read and discuss the questions with your class.

1. Who has the most serious problem because the flights are delayed?

2. Who does not fly very often?

3. Who is the most relaxed of the five passengers?

STRUCTURE AND PRONUNCIATION

A **Present Continuous Tense**   Choose the correct verb from the box and complete the sentences in the present continuous tense.

stand	get
take off	send
talk	read
rain	sit
cry	

1. Sarah _____ the newspaper.
2. It _____ very hard.
3. Samip _____ at the car rental counter.
4. The secretary _____ the papers now.
5. People _____ their shoes.
6. People _____ upset.
7. The plane _____ here on the runway.
8. One kid _____.
9. Carly _____ to all her friends.

B **Dictation**   Listen and copy the sentences you hear.

CD 2; Track 10

1. _____
2. _____
3. _____
4. _____
5. _____

C **Expressions**   Complete the sentences with the expressions you hear.

CD 2; Track 11

Pronunciation Note

When people are speaking, they use expressions such as *ah, uh-huh, okay, I know, good, yeah,* and *You're right* to show that they are listening or to agree with the speaker.

1. I'm renting a car . . . _____ . . . _____, they have a car.
2. _____, _____, it's Bobby's wedding.
3. _____, _____. Flying is no fun.
4. _____, I will. I'll get something to eat.
5. And the reports? . . . _____ . . . _____. So you're sending them out now. _____. _____.

LISTENING 2: AIRPORT ANNOUNCEMENTS

A Match   Read each statement below and talk about any new words. Then, listen and write the number of each announcement next to the correct statement.

CD 2; Track 12

_____ a. We are canceling the flight because of bad weather.

_____ b. It is time to get on the plane.

_____ c. The plane can't take off on time. The flight is delayed.

___1___ d. We are looking for a passenger.

_____ e. We are changing the gate for this flight.

_____ f. There are too many passengers on this flight. Can you change your plans and leave later?

B Listen and Complete   Listen again and complete the announcements with the correct answers.

CD 2; Track 12

1. Attention, please. Paging Mr. Julio Vargas. Please report to Gate _____.

2. Good evening, ladies and gentlemen. Flight _____ to Miami is now boarding. We are boarding rows 20 to 25.

3. All passengers for Flight _____ to Denver, Colorado. It is snowing in Denver and the Denver airport has been closed. Due to the bad weather, we are canceling Flight _____.

4. Passengers on Flight _____, this flight is overbooked. We are looking for two passengers to change their flights. We are offering first class seats on the next flight to Boston. That flight leaves in _____ hours. You will also receive a voucher for _____ to use on a future flight.

5. Passengers on Flight 449 to London, there is a gate change. The flight is not leaving from Terminal A, Gate 25. Please go to Terminal _____. Flight 449 is leaving from Terminal _____, Gate _____.

6. Ladies and gentlemen, because of the rain, Flight _____ scheduled to leave at _____ is delayed. The new departure time is _____.

SPEAKING

A **Write**   Work in a small group and write two rules or regulations for each of these locations in an airport.

Ticket counter:

You have to show a license or passport.

You can only take two bags.

Security:

_____

_____

Boarding Gate:

_____

_____

Customs:

_____

_____

B **Partner Practice**   Sit with a partner and complete this conversation at immigration/passport control.

A: What country are you from?

B: _____.

A: What is the purpose for your visit?

B: _____.

A: Where are you staying?

B: _____.

A: How long are you going to stay?

B: _____.

EDUARDO

BEFORE YOU LISTEN

A Discuss   Talk about these questions.

1. Do you write or e-mail family and friends in your native country?

2. Are you going to visit or return to your native country at some time in the future? What are your plans?

3. How much is an airline ticket from here to your country?

B Read   Read about Eduardo. Underline any new words.

Eduardo

Eduardo is looking at his airline ticket again and smiling. Tomorrow he's going to be with his family in Cartagena. He's going to leave the snow and cold of New York for the hot sun of his native Colombia.

Eduardo left Columbia about three years ago. He rents a small apartment. He goes to school and he works six or seven days a week. He has a big TV, a car, and nice clothes. But he's lonely, very lonely.

Eduardo is packing his suitcase. He's looking at a picture of Yolanda. Yolanda and he went to the same high school together in Colombia and their parents are good friends. They've been writing letters and e-mails for two years. At first, they wrote as friends. But now, their letters are more romantic. When Eduardo gets to Colombia, he is going to spend a lot of time with Yolanda. How is Eduardo going to feel about Yolanda? How is Yolanda going to feel about Eduardo?

Listening Note

When you listen to a story or conversation, it is easier to follow when you know something about the speaker. You can make predictions about what the speaker might say or do. As you follow the story, you can check your predictions.

C Predict   What are your predictions about Eduardo and Yolanda?

LISTENING 1: STORY

CD 2; Track 13

A **First Listening**   You will hear four conversations. As you listen, decide who is talking and complete the information under each picture.

1. _____ is talking

   to _____.

2. _____ is talking

   to _____.

3. _____ is talking

   to _____.

4. _____ is talking

   to _____.

B **Listen for Information**   Listen to each conversation again. After you listen, tell the class any information you remember about the speakers.

C **Who Is Talking?** Read each sentence and circle the letter of the correct person. Circle *E* for Eduardo, *Y* for Yolanda, *M* for mother, or *F* for father.

1. I can't stay here.   E Y M F

2. What are you going to do if you have a baby? E Y M F

3. I don't want you to leave.   E Y M F

4. I can see you love him in your eyes and in   E Y M F
   your smile.

5. I want you to think about it.   E Y M F

6. When are we going to see you again?   E Y M F

7. It's my last day of work for one month.   E Y M F

8. Yes, I have to learn English.   E Y M F

9. I have to leave next week.   E Y M F

10. Follow your heart.   E Y M F

CD 2; Track 14

D **Listen and Circle** Listen to Yolanda speak with her mother. Yolanda's mother is worried about her daughter leaving home. What are some of her worries? Listen and circle the things that Yolanda's mother spoke about.

1. Yolanda's mother is going to miss her.

2. Yolanda's family and friends are in Colombia.

3. Yolanda doesn't speak English.

4. Yolanda does not know Eduardo very well.

5. Yolanda and Eduardo's children will be Americans.

6. Life in the United States is expensive.

7. She cannot help Yolanda if she has children.

8. Eduardo is older than Yolanda.

E **What do you think?** Read and discuss the questions with your class.

1. Do you think that Yolanda should marry Eduardo?

2. Who is more realistic, Yolanda's mother or father? Who is more romantic?

3. Do you believe that people should "follow their hearts" when they are in love?

STRUCTURE AND PRONUNCIATION

A Future Tense Choose the correct verb from the box and complete the sentences in the future tense.

return	ask
fly	leave
see	visit
spend	stay
talk	be

1. Eduardo _**is going to leave**_ tomorrow.
2. He _____ to Colombia.
3. He _____ there for one month.
4. He _____ his family and friends.
5. They _____ happy to see him.
6. He _____ a lot of time with Yolanda.
7. They _____ about the future.
8. They _____ her family.
9. Eduardo _____ to New York next month.
10. Eduardo _____ Yolanda to marry him.

B Dictation Listen and write the questions you hear.

CD 2; Track 15

1. _____
2. _____
3. _____
4. _____
5. _____

C "Going to" Listen and repeat the sentences below. Then, sit with a partner and practice the sentences together.

CD 2; Track 16

> ## Pronunciation Note
> In conversational English, *going to* often sounds like *gonna*.
> Note: Always write *going to*. Do not write *gonna*.

1. Eduardo and Yolanda are going to get married.
2. He's going to give her a ring.
3. Yolanda is going to plan the wedding.
4. Eduardo is going to return to Colombia in four months.
5. They are going to have a big wedding.
6. Eduardo is going to return to the United States with Yolanda.

LISTENING 2: CONVERSATIONS

CD 2; Track 17

Ⓐ Listen and Write the Number   Yolanda and Eduardo are in love. They are talking about life in the United States. Listen to the two conversations. Write the number of each conversation next to Yolanda's feelings.

_____ a. Yolanda wants to marry Eduardo and come to the United States.

_____ b. Yolanda isn't sure she wants to leave Colombia. She is worried about life in the United States.

Ⓑ Read and Discuss   Read the description of an optimist and a pessimist. Which are you?

I studied hard. I'm going to do great on the test.

I studied hard. I'm going to fail the test.

An **optimist** looks on the positive side of life. This person looks at the future and expects good things to happen.

A **pessimist** looks at the negative side of life. This person looks at the future and expects bad things to happen.

Ⓒ Listen and Circle   Listen to each statement from Eduardo. Is Yolanda an optimist or a pessimist in each reply? Circle *optimist* or *pessimist*.

CD 2; Track 18

1. You have to learn English.   (optimist)   pessimist
2. You'll miss your family.   optimist   pessimist
3. I have a car. I'll teach you to drive. optimist   pessimist
4. All your friends are here.   optimist   pessimist
5. You'll want to find a job.   optimist   pessimist
6. It's very cold in the winter.   optimist   pessimist
7. I work all day.   optimist   pessimist
8. New York is a big city.   optimist   pessimist

SPEAKING

A Write   Your cousin is planning to come to live in the United States. Work in a small group. Write and tell her about four things she is going to like. Then, write and tell her about four things she is not going to like.

Things she is going to like:

1. _____

2. _____

3. _____

4. _____

Things she isn't going to like:

1. _____

2. _____

3. _____

4. _____

B Discuss   Sit in a group and read each situation. What would an optimist say? What would a pessimist say?

1. We have a big test next week.

2. I'm going to take my driving test next week.

3. A new Mexican restaurant just opened in town.

4. We are going to have a new teacher in the next class.

5. My friend is going to move to Chicago next month.

6. Our teacher was absent yesterday.

7. Let's go to the beach tomorrow.

8. The bus is late.

9. My boss just retired. The new boss starts tomorrow.

10. I'm having problems with my car. It's at the service center now.

THE DIVORCE

BEFORE YOU LISTEN

A **Discuss**   Talk about the questions.

1. Do you know anyone who is divorced?

2. Do they have children?

3. Do the children live with their mother or with their father?

4. How often do they see the other parent?

B **Parenting Plan**   When parents divorce, family counselors suggest that they make a parenting plan to decide on the children's schedule, education, and health. As a class, list five things that a good parenting plan should include.

1. _____**If possible, the children should stay in the same school.**_____

2. _____

3. _____

4. _____

5. _____

C **Key Words**   Talk about the new words. Then, complete the sentences.

far	anymore	anytime	near	argue	together

1. My sister and her husband _____ about money, the car, the children, everything.

2. They aren't in love with each other _____.

3. Their parents are living _____ away in another state.

4. You can call me _____ ; I'll always have time to talk to you.

5. My sister lives _____ me in the same town.

6. We're going on vacation _____ in the summer.

A.

B.

C.

D.

E.

F.

G.

H.

LISTENING 1: STORY

Listening Note

Before you listen, think about the topic. What do you already know about it? What are your ideas about the topic? As you listen, you can compare your ideas with the story.

CD 2; Track 19

A First Listening   Tom and Marsha are telling their children that they are going to get a divorce and are talking about the boys' future. Look at the picture and listen to the story. After you listen, tell the class any information you remember. Look back at your parenting plan on page 43. Which of your ideas are talked about in the story?

CD 2; Track 20

B Listen and Choose   Listen and write the letter of the correct picture.

1. _____   3. _____   5. _____   7. _____

2. _____   4. _____   6. _____   8. _____

CD 2; Track 21

C Comprehension Questions   Listen and circle the correct answer.

1. a. a new school
   b. the same school
   c. I don't know

2. a. this weekend
   b. today
   c. this summer

3. a. to the next town
   b. next door
   c. to the beach

4. a. two weekends a month
   b. anytime
   c. in his apartment

5. a. every weekend
   b. twice a month
   c. anytime

6. a. upset
   b. happy
   c. tired

D What do you think?   Read and discuss the questions with your class.

1. What are some reasons that couples get divorced? Do we know why Marsha and Tom are getting divorced?

2. What are some of the biggest changes in a child's life after a divorce?

3. What other plans do these parents need to make for their children?

STRUCTURE AND PRONUNCIATION

CD 2; Track 22

A **Tense Contrast**   Listen and decide if the statement is about right now or the future. Circle *right now* or *future.*

1. right now   future
2. right now   future
3. right now   future
4. right now   future
5. right now   future

6. right now   future
7. right now   future
8. right now   future
9. right now   future
10. right now   future

CD 2; Track 23

B **Dictation**   Listen and write the sentences you hear. All of the sentences are about the future time. Remember that in spoken English, *going to* sounds like *gonna.*

1. _____
2. _____
3. _____
4. _____
5. _____

CD 2; Track 24

C **Time Expressions**   Listen to the sentences. Fill in the time expression.

1. The boys are going to see their father **two weekends a month** .
2. They can call him _____ .
3. They're going to go on vacation _____ .
4. Tom and Marsha argue _____ .
5. Tom is going to leave _____ .
6. He's going to move _____ .
7. The boys are going to see their father _____ .
8. They're going to call their father _____ .
9. Marsha is going to talk to a lawyer _____ .
10. The boys are going to go to the same school _____ .

LISTENING 2: CONVERSATIONS

 Ⓐ Match   Listen to each argument. Decide what the man and woman are arguing about. Write the number of each conversation near the correct picture.

CD 2; Track 25

 Ⓑ Word Stress   Listen and circle the word or words that are stressed.

CD 2; Track 26

 Pronunciation Note

Stress
The most important words in a sentence are stressed. These words are the longest and loudest in the sentence.
Example: You [never] do [anything.]

1. You always say that.
2. You do nothing.
3. How are we going to pay the rent?
4. You bought a new coat.
5. I needed a coat.

6. And I needed a camera.
7. 11:00 isn't too late for a 16-year-old.
8. I don't want her out this late.
9. You never think about me.
10. It's always what you want.

SPEAKING

Ⓐ Partner Practice   In each short conversation, two people are arguing. Sit with a partner and practice these conversations together. Stress the most important words.

1. A: I can't help you.

   B: Why not?

   A: I'm tired.

   B: You're always tired.

2. A: You never help with the shopping.

   B: I hate the supermarket.

   A: I don't like it, either.

   B: I'll come next time.

   A: That's your favorite expression. Next time.

3. A: What's for dinner?

   B: I don't know.

   A: You don't know?

   B: I'm not cooking.

   A: You're not?

   B: I cleaned all day. You watched TV. Now, I think I'll watch TV.

Ⓑ List   List six common things that couples argue about. Sit with a partner and share your ideas.

1. _____   3. _____   5. _____

2. _____   4. _____   6. _____

Ⓒ Act It Out   Who do you argue with . . . someone in your family? a friend? a neighbor? Complete the sentences and share the information with your partner.

A. I sometimes argue with my _____ .
   We argue about _____ .

B. I sometimes argue with my _____ .
   We argue about _____ .

Then, with your partner, write a short argument between two people. Present it to the class. The class will try to guess who is arguing: a parent and child, two neighbors, a brother and sister, a husband and wife, etc.

MY FAMILY

BEFORE YOU LISTEN

Ⓐ Discuss   Talk about the questions.

1. Where were you born? Do you still live in the same country?

2. Do you live with your parents? If not, where do your parents live?

3. Do you have any relatives who live in another country?

4. Did you ever travel to another country? Where did you go?

Ⓑ Family Vocabulary   Cross out the word that does not belong.

1. a. divorced   b. married   c. separated   d. photographs

2. a. stepmother   b. brother   c. stepsister   d. stepfather

3. a. holiday   b. engaged   c. fiancé   d. wedding

4. a. pregnant   b. visit   c. baby   d. expecting

5. a. sister   b. brother   c. teacher   d. family

Ⓒ Key Words   Talk about the new words. Complete the sentences.

wedding	army	keep in touch	pregnant
graduate	grade	hotel management	

1. My brother is a soldier in the _____. He is serving in Korea.

2. My best friend is getting married next month and I'm in the _____.

3. I'm majoring in _____ because I want to work for a large hotel.

4. My little sister is in elementary school. She's in the first _____.

5. I'm a college student in the United States. I _____ with my family in Japan by e-mail.

6. My sister is _____. She's going to have a little girl.

7. I'm going to _____ from college next year.

LISTENING 1: STORY

A First Listening Look at the photographs and listen to the conversation. As you listen, write the name of each person under the correct picture. After you listen, tell the class any information you can remember about each person in the photographs.

Katrina	Oscar	Sarah
Ashley	Tony	Jenny

B Complete   Listen and complete the chart about this family. Write the relationship and the country where each person is living.

CD 3; Track 1

Name	Relationship to speaker	Country
Katrina		
Oscar		
Sarah		
Ashley		
Tony		
Katie		
Jenny		

C Fill In   Complete the sentences about this family.

1. In the summer, the speaker lives with her _____.

2. On the holidays, she visits her _____.

3. Last summer, she went to China and lived with her _____.

4. This summer, her _____ is getting married.

5. Her _____ is a teacher.

6. Her _____ is in the third grade.

7. Her _____ is in the army.

Listening Note

Between friends, listeners take an active part in the conversation by asking questions and making comments.

D Active Listening   Read the statements. Then, listen to the questions and match each with the correct answer or response.

CD 3; Track 2

____ a. In the summer.

____ b. Yes, I visited her last summer.

____ c. Yes, that's Jenny. She has short black hair and glasses, like me.

____ d. Hmm-hmm. That's Dad.

____ e. That's my brother, Antonio, but everyone calls him Tony.

____ f. He lives in Houston and works for a bank there.

_1_ g. Yes, that's my mom.

STRUCTURE AND PRONUNCIATION

A Present Tense   Choose the correct verb from the box and complete the sentences in the simple present tense.

call   have
wear   live
be   work
keep

1. My father _____ **lives** _____ in Houston.
2. My brother _____ in the army.
3. Everyone _____ him Tony.
4. My sister _____ short black hair.
5. She _____ glasses.
6. Her husband _____ for a company in China.
7. They _____ in Beijing.
8. We _____ in touch by e-mail.

B Dictation   Listen and copy the sentences you hear.

CD 3; Track 3

1. _____
2. _____
3. _____
4. _____
5. _____

C Linking   Listen and mark the linking sounds. Then, listen again and repeat the sentences.

CD 3; Track 4

Pronunciation Note

Many words in English are linked, or joined, together. Put the final consonant of a word together with the next vowel.

She's a teacher.   She lives in Mexico.

1. She's American.
2. They have a little girl.
3. She's eight.
4. She's in third grade.
5. He lives in Houston.
6. He works in a bank.
7. He's in the army.
8. They live in Beijing.
9. We keep in touch by e-mail.
10. I'd like to work in a hotel.

Sit with a partner and practice saying the sentences, linking the words.

LISTENING 2: CONVERSATIONS

CD 3; Track 5

(A) Match Listen to each conversation. Write the number of each conversation under the correct picture.

a. _____ b. _____ c. _____

CD 3; Track 5

(B) Answer Listen to the conversations again. Answer the questions.

Conversation 1:

   1. How often does this woman see her granddaughter?

   2. How long will they be in California?

Conversation 2:

   1. Are these two women good friends?

   2. Why does the mother-in-law pick up the boys after school?

Conversation 3:

   1. Where do you think the speakers are?

   2. How well do these two men know each other?

   3. How many children does each man have?

SPEAKING

(A) Discuss Sit in a small group and talk about your families.

1. How many brothers and sisters do you have? Are you the oldest, youngest, or in the middle?

2. Do your brothers and sisters live in this country?

3. Where are your parents? Do they work? What do they do?

4. Are you married? If so, how long have you been married?

5. How many children do you have?

6. How often do you see your family?

7. How do you keep in touch with your family?

CD 3; Track 6

B **Listen and Write**   Sit with a partner. Listen and write questions we often ask when looking at photographs.

Photos of Children:

1. _____

2. _____

3. _____

Photos of Adults:

1. _____

2. _____

3. _____

4. _____

5. _____

Show your partner pictures of your family. Use the questions above to ask about family members.

C **Conversations**   Look at the photographs below. Make up conversations about the women in each of the photographs.

Example: A: Who's that young woman wearing a sun hat?

B: That's my next door neighbor, Millie.

THE SUNSET MOTEL

BEFORE YOU LISTEN

A Discuss   Talk about the questions.

1. When you travel, where do you like to stay?

2. What hotel do you like? What services do they offer?

3. When is the last time you stayed at a hotel/motel? What did you like about your stay? What didn't you like?

B Check   You are driving a long distance and you need to stay at a motel. Check three things that are important to you in choosing a place to stay.

☐   1. It's near the highway.   ☐   6. It has a restaurant.

☐   2. It's cheap.   ☐   7. It has room service.

☐   3. It's clean.   ☐   8. It has a telephone.

☐   4. It has a pool.   ☐   9. It has a television.

☐   5. It's in a quiet area.   ☐ 10. It has Internet service.

C Key Words   Talk about the new words. Complete the sentences.

| mistakes   employees   dependable   minimum wage   complains |

1. Two _____ of the motel are a desk clerk and a housekeeper.

2. The _____ is the lowest salary a company can pay its employees.

3. The boss fired the worker after she made too many _____.

4. A _____ worker comes to work on time.

5. The boss is never happy with our work. He _____ about everyone!

LISTENING 1: STORY

CD 3; Track 7

A **First Listening**   Listen to the first part of this story. It gives a description of the Sunset Motel. Check the services and amenities that the motel offers.

____ 1. pool

____ 2. gift shop

____ 3. restaurant

____ 4. a television in each room

____ 5. a telephone in each room

____ 6. Internet service

____ 7. exercise room

JACK   MABEL   MR. HIGGINS

CD 3; Track 8

B **Write the Name** Listen to the description of the hotel, the employees and the owner. Write the name of the correct person: Jack, Mabel, or Mr. Higgins.

1. _____ cleans the rooms.

2. _____ sometimes comes late.

3. _____ makes a lot of mistakes on the bills.

4. _____ complains all the time.

5. _____ registers guests.

6. _____ only pays the minimum wage.

7. _____ never checks the closets.

8. _____ isn't easy to work for.

9. _____ is friendly to all the guests.

10. _____ sometimes gives people the wrong key.

Listening Note
After making a statement, a speaker often follows it with an example.

CD 3; Track 9

C **Match** Read the examples below. Then, listen to each statement. Match the statement and the example.

____ a. She often comes late.

_1_ b. If a guest is staying in room 11, he gives them the key for room 12.

____ c. He only pays the minimum wage.

____ d. Sometimes she forgets to put clean towels in the bathroom.

____ e. They drive in late at night and leave early the next morning.

____ f. If the bill is $59, he charges $49.

____ g. He isn't friendly and he doesn't smile.

____ h. A room is only $59 a night.

D **What do you think?** Discuss the questions with your class.

1. Who stops at the motel?

2. Why does Mr. Higgins have a difficult time keeping his employees?

3. Would you apply for a job at this motel? Why or why not?

STRUCTURE AND PRONUNCIATION

A **Present Tense**   Choose the correct verb from the box and complete the sentences in the present tense. Some of the sentences are negative.

give	come
need	register
pay	put
have	complain

1. The motel **doesn't have** a pool.

2. Jack Jones _____ guests.

3. Sometimes, Jack _____ the guest the right key.

4. Sometimes, Mabel _____ to work.

5. Sometimes, she _____ clean towels in the bathroom.

6. Mr. Higgins _____ more dependable workers.

7. He always _____ about everything.

8. He _____ his employees well.

CD 3; Track 10

B **Dictation**   Listen and copy the sentences you hear.

1. _____

2. _____

3. _____

4. _____

5. _____

CD 3; Track 11

C **Contractions**   Listen and repeat the sentences. Then, sit with a partner and read the sentences to one another. Be careful of the pronunciation of the contractions.

> ### Pronunciation Note
> Negative contractions end in '*t*, for example, *isn't* and *doesn't*. These contractions have two syllables, but the final *t* is not strong.

1. The motel isn't in a city.
2. The area isn't noisy.
3. The motel isn't expensive.
4. The motel doesn't have a pool.
5. The owner isn't friendly.
6. He doesn't smile at people.
7. He isn't easy to work for.

LISTENING 2: CONVERSATIONS

A **Answer the Questions**   Mr. Higgins is interviewing Carla for the desk clerk job. Listen and answer the questions.

1. How many rooms does Sunset Motel have?

2. What computer system does Sunset Motel use?

3. What hours does Mr. Higgins need Carla?

4. How long is the dinner break?

5. What days does Mr. Higgins need a desk clerk?

6. What is the pay? What is the overtime pay?

Listening Note

You will often hear people repeat information. They want to be sure that they understand the information or that their information is correct.

B **Repeating Information**   To be sure that she has the information correct, Carla repeats several things that Mr. Higgins says. Listen again and complete the sentences.

1. CARLA: How large is your motel?

   MR. HIGGINS: We have twelve rooms.

   CARLA: _____.

2. CARLA: What computer system do you use?

   MR. H: We don't have a computer in the office.
   We do everything by hand.

   CARLA: _____.

3. CARLA: What are the hours?

   MR. H: 1:00 to 9:00.

   CARLA: _____.
   And how long is the dinner break?

   MR. H: The dinner break? There's no dinner break.

   CARLA: _____?

   MR. H: You can eat your dinner at the desk.

4. CARLA: That's 48 hours a week. What is the pay?

   MR. H: I pay minimum wage.

   CARLA: _____?!

SPEAKING

A Partner Practice   Work in pairs to practice repeating information. One student is the boss (Keep your book open and look at sentences 1 to 10 below). The other student is interviewing for a job (Close your book). The boss is speaking about the job. Student 2 will repeat the information. Use the exact words or words that are similar.

Example: Student 1 (Looking at book):
            Work begins at 7:00 a.m.
            Student 2 (Book closed):
            Work begins at 7:00 a.m. *Or*
            Okay. 7:00 a.m.

1. Work begins at 7:00 a.m.

2. If you are late three times, you lose the job.

3. We're closed on Sunday and Monday.

4. Wear black pants and a white shirt.

5. Wear your name tag.

6. There's a fifteen-minute break at 9:00.

7. Lunch is at 12:00.

8. You have thirty minutes for lunch.

9. The pay is $10.00 an hour.

10. When you work overtime, the pay is $15.00 an hour.

B Job Interview   With a partner, prepare a job interview between the boss of a delivery company and a person looking for a job. Use the questions to help you. Two groups can present their interviews to the class.

Tell me about yourself. Tell me about your experience.

Why did you leave your last job?

Why do you want to work for this company?

Did you ever work as a driver before?

Do you have a clean driving record?

How well do you know this area?

Are you available nights and weekends?

What languages can you speak?

ALASKA

BEFORE YOU LISTEN

A Discuss   Look at a map of the United States. Discuss the questions.

1. How many states are there in the United States?

2. Forty-eight states are part of the continental United States. Two states are separate. What are they?

3. What is the largest state? How big is it?

4. Which states have you visited?

B Key Words   Talk about the new words. Complete the sentences.

population	rises	sets	pipeline	tourists
glacier	distance	oil	wildlife	seaport

1. A _____ is a river of ice.

2. You can see bears, whales and other _____ in Alaska.

3. The _____ of Barrow is 4,500 people.

4. Many people use _____ to heat their houses.

5. A _____ carries oil from one place to another.

6. A _____ is a safe place for large ships.

7. In the morning, the sun _____ at about 6:30. In the evening, the sun _____ at about 7:00.

8. The _____ from New York to California is about 3,000 miles.

9. The _____ enjoyed their vacation in Alaska.

C More Key Words   Circle the names of the fish or animals. Put a line under the activities.

hike	eagle	take a cruise	bear
whale	salmon	kayak	bike

D Reading a Map Look at the map of Alaska and complete the information.

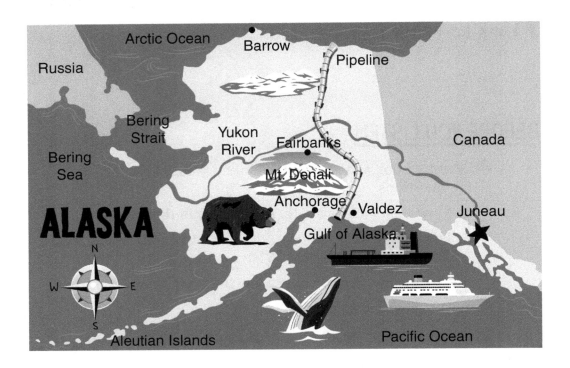

1. The capital of Alaska is _____.

2. The _____ Ocean borders Alaska to the south. The _____ Ocean borders Alaska to the north.

3. _____ borders Alaska to the east.

4. _____ is across the Bering Strait from Alaska.

5. The _____ River runs through the middle of Alaska.

6. _____ is the tallest mountain in Alaska.

7. The northernmost city in Alaska is _____.

8. The _____ carries oil from Prudhoe Bay in the north to _____, a seaport in the southern part of the state.

What other information do you know from looking at this map?

LISTENING 1: STORY

Listening Note

In a talk about a country or state, you will hear information about size, location, borders, population, the capital, important cities, transportation, industries, and weather. A map can give you some of this information before you listen. Looking at a map while you listen will help you follow the talk.

A First Listening   Listen to the information about Alaska. As you listen, point to each place on the map. After you listen, tell the class any information that you remember.

CD 3; Track 13

B Follow the Speaker   Listen again to the talk about Alaska and follow the outline below. As you listen, put a check mark in each box as the speaker talks about it.

CD 3; Track 13

☐ A. Size   ☐ E. Important cities

☐ B. Location   ☐ F. Transportation

☐ C. Borders   ☐ G. Important industries

☐ D. Population   ☐ H. Weather

C Listen and Circle   Circle the answer for each statement. Compare your answers with a partner. Then, listen and check your answers.

CD 3; Track 13

1. The population of Alaska is about _____ people.
   a. 6,700   b. 67,000   c. 670,000

2. About half the people in Alaska live in _____.
   a. Anchorage   b. Juneau   c. Barrow

3. If you want to visit Juneau, you have to _____ there.
   a. drive   b. fly   c. take a train

4. The coldest city in Alaska is _____.
   a. Juneau   b. Valdez   c. Barrow

5. Because Alaska is so large, many people travel by _____.
   a. car   b. train   c. plane

6. Alaska's largest industry is _____.
   a. oil   b. tourism   c. fishing

7. Ships bring oil from _____ to seaports in the United States.
   a. Barrow   b. Anchorage   c. Valdez

STRUCTURE AND PRONUNCIATION

A Present Tense   Choose the correct verb from the box and complete the sentences in the present tense.

set	visit
produce	rain
rise	have
carry	live
drive	take

1. Alaska _____**has**_____ many long rivers.
2. In Barrow, the sun _____ on May 10th.
3. In Barrow, the sun _____ on November 18th.
4. Some people _____ on ice roads in the winter.
5. About half the people in Alaska _____ in Anchorage.
6. Alaska _____ 7 percent of the oil used in the United States.
7. The pipeline _____ oil from Prudhoe Bay to Valdez.
8. Ships _____ the oil to other seaports.
9. Thousands of tourists _____ Alaska each year.
10. It _____ several days a week in the summer.

B Pronunciation   Listen and repeat each superlative adjective.

CD 3; Track 14

1. the largest
2. the smallest
3. the best
4. the coldest
5. the biggest
6. the tallest
7. the longest
8. the most

C Dictation   Listen and complete the sentences. Each sentence uses an adjective from Exercise B. Then, listen again and repeat the sentences.

CD 3; Track 15

1. Alaska _____
2. The Yukon is _____
3. Mt. Denali _____
4. Barrow is _____
5. _____
6. _____

LISTENING 2: CONVERSATIONS

Ⓐ Expand Your Vocabulary   Write two words you think of for each season.

Winter	Spring	Summer	Fall
_____	_____	_____	_____
_____	_____	_____	_____

CD 3; Track 16

Ⓑ Complete the Chart   Listen and complete the chart with a few notes. What season(s) does each person like? What is the reason?

Speaker	Favorite Season	Reason
1. Matt		
2. Cindy		
3. Sam		
4. Lauri		

Ⓒ Match   Look at the chart in Exercise B and write the name of the correct person under each picture. Then, talk about the pictures.

1. _____

3. _____

2. _____

4. _____

SPEAKING

A Discuss   In a small group, talk about the seasons.

1. What kind of weather do you like?

2. What is your favorite season? Why?

3. What outdoor activities do you enjoy?

4. For the weather, where is the best place to live in this country? Why?

B Drawing a Map   Your class will discuss the state or a country in which you live. First, draw an outline of your state or country on a plain piece of paper. Then, add the following features to your map.

1. the borders

2. the capital (put a small star in front of the capital)

3. two large cities

4. the longest river and the tallest mountain

5. one interesting feature

6. a place you like to visit or want to visit

7. a small smiling face to show your location

C Complete   Look at your map and complete the information.

1. I live in _____.

2. The capital is _____.

3. The population is about _____ people.

4. The tallest mountain is _____.

5. The longest river is _____.

6. Two large cities are _____ and

_____.

7. Two important industries are _____

and _____.

8. An interesting place to visit is _____.

9. The best time to visit is _____ because

the weather is _____.

GOOD HEALTH

BEFORE YOU LISTEN

A Discuss   Talk about the questions.

1. What is a heart attack? What are the causes?
2. Do you know anyone who had a heart attack?
3. What are the causes of a heart attack?

B Checklist   Heart attack is a leading cause of death in the United States for both men and women. Heart attacks are caused by a number of factors. How many of these factors do you have?

1. Do you smoke?   Yes   No
2. Do you have high cholesterol?   Yes   No
3. Do you have high blood pressure?   Yes   No
4. Do you have diabetes?   Yes   No
5. Are you overweight?   Yes   No
6. Do you have a lot of stress?   Yes   No
7. Do you need to exercise more?   Yes   No
8. Do you have a family history of heart attacks?   Yes   No

C Key Words   Talk about the new words. Then, complete the sentences.

| except | miss | increase | cardiac care unit | dizzy |

1. I can't drink caffeine anymore. I really _____ a cup of coffee in the morning.

2. Many hospitals have a _____ to care for patients with heart problems.

3. No one in my family smokes, _____ me.

4. You can walk one mile the first month. The second month, you can _____ that to two miles.

5. When it's very hot in a room, I sometimes feel _____.

LISTENING 1: STORY

CD 3; Track 17

Ⓐ First Listening   Look at the pictures and listen to the story about Len. Then, tell the class any information you remember.

   Listening Note

Sometimes, a speaker gives several facts, instructions, or directions. To help people follow the ideas, speakers use words like *First, Second, Next, Then,* and *Finally.*

CD 3; Track 17

Ⓑ Complete   Listen to the talk again. Len needs to make four changes to his lifestyle. Listen and complete the sentences.

1. First, Len needs to _____.

2. Second, Len needs to _____.

3. Next, Len has to _____.

4. Finally, Len has to _____.

CD 3; Track 18

Ⓒ Listen and Write the Letter   Listen to the sentences. Write the letter of the correct picture.

1. _____   3. _____   5. _____   7. _____

2. _____   4. _____   6. _____   8. _____

CD 3; Track 19

Ⓓ Comprehension Questions   Listen and circle the correct answer.

1. a. He's sick.
   b. He's 50.
   c. Yes, he is.

2. a. He had a heart attack.
   b. It was his birthday.
   c. He was leaving his office.

3. a. at his office
   b. at home
   c. at the hospital

4. a. one day
   b. two weeks
   c. for two months

5. a. steak
   b. vegetables
   c. fish

6. a. before work
   b. after work
   c. before and after work

7. a. four
   b. seven
   c. eight

Ⓔ What do you think?   Discuss the questions with your class.

1. Why did Len have a heart attack?

2. What does this sentence mean, "He remembers the faces of his wife and daughters in the emergency room"?

3. Why do you think that so many Americans die from heart problems? What is the leading cause of death in your native country?

STRUCTURE AND PRONUNCIATION

A Has to, Can, Can't Listen to these sentences. Write the complete verb you hear. Listen for *has to, can,* or *can't.*

CD 3; Track 20

Examples: A: He _____**has to watch**_____ his diet.

B: He _____**can eat**_____ chicken and fish.

C: He _____**can't eat**_____ steak.

1. He _____ weight.

2. He _____ regular coffee.

3. He _____ decaf coffee.

4. He _____ before and after work.

5. He _____ anymore.

6. He _____ at the office.

7. He _____ ten hours a day anymore.

B Dictation Listen and copy the sentences you hear.

CD 3; Track 21

1. _____

2. _____

3. _____

4. _____

5. _____

C Can / Can't Listen to these sentences. Complete with *can* or *can't.*

CD 3; Track 22

Pronunciation Note

can and *can't*

Can is pronounced *can.* The main verb is stressed.

He can walk one mile a day.

Can't is pronounced *can't.* We often don't hear the *t.*

Both *can't* and the main verb are stressed.

He can't put salt on his food.

1. I _____ eat dairy products.

2. I _____ eat anything I want.

3. I _____ lose weight.

4. I _____ relax.

5. I _____ do 25 pushups.

LISTENING 2: CONVERSATIONS

 A Match Len is at the doctor for his three-month checkup. Listen to these conversations between Len and his doctor. Write the number of each conversation on the correct picture.

CD 3; Track 23

 B Answer the Questions Listen to the conversations again. Answer the questions with the class.

CD 3; Track 23

1. How many more hours can Len work this month?

2. How many cups of regular coffee can Len have a day?

3. How many minutes will it take Len to walk two miles?

4. What does the doctor mean when he says, "You were lucky this time."?

5. How high is Len's cholesterol now? How high should it be?

6. How many times a day should Len take his medication?

 C Listen and Complete Listen to the doctor's orders and complete the sentences. When should you take the medication?

CD 3; Track 24

1. Take this _____ a day.

2. Take _____ tablet _____ each meal.

3. Take _____ tablet every _____ hours as needed for pain.

4. Take _____ tablets now, then _____ tablet _____ times a day.

5. Take _____ tablet _____ hour _____ each meal.

SPEAKING

CD 3; Track 25

Ⓐ Listen and Answer   Listen to the conversation between a patient and doctor who is prescribing some medication. Answer the questions.

1. How will this medication help the patient?

2. How long will the patient need to take it?

3. How often should he take it?

4. What are the side effects?

5. Will his insurance cover the medication?

6. Can he take a generic brand of this drug?

Ⓑ Act It Out   Write a conversation between a doctor and a patient about a medication the doctor is prescribing. Use the questions in Exercise A to help you. Two or three groups should act out their conversations for the class.

Ⓒ Label Warnings   Sit in a group. Read the warnings. Say each warning in your own words.

1. Keep out of reach of children.

2. Do not drink alcohol while taking this medication.

3. Stop taking this medication if you become pregnant.

4. Shake well before using.

Ⓓ Read the Label   Read the label and look at each picture. What is the person doing wrong?

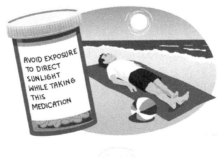

FAST THINKING

BEFORE YOU LISTEN

A Discuss   Talk about the questions.

1. Did anyone ever rob you? Where were you?

2. What did the person steal?

3. Did you call the police? What did they do?

4. What do you think are some of the most common items that people steal?

B Complete   Complete the sentences with rob or steal.

> *Rob* means to take *from*. You rob a person or a place, e.g. a blank, a store. *Steal* means to take. You steal items, such as money, jewelry, and computers.   rob — robbed   steal — stole

1. Someone _____ my laptop from my dormitory.

2. A thief _____ the bank. He _____ $5,000.

3. A man _____ my bag when I was coming out of the store.

4. Last night, someone _____ the jewelry store in town.

C Key Words   Talk about the new words. Then, complete the sentences.

focused	purse	jail	robbery	scream	arrested

1. Last night, there was a _____ at our friend's house.

2. The police _____ the man who stole my money.

3. She _____ the camera to get a better picture of the children.

4. I jumped out of bed when I heard a loud _____ .

5. My neighbor is serving one year in _____ for stealing a car.

6. A woman keeps many things in her _____ — keys, a wallet, cell phone, make up, and sunglasses.

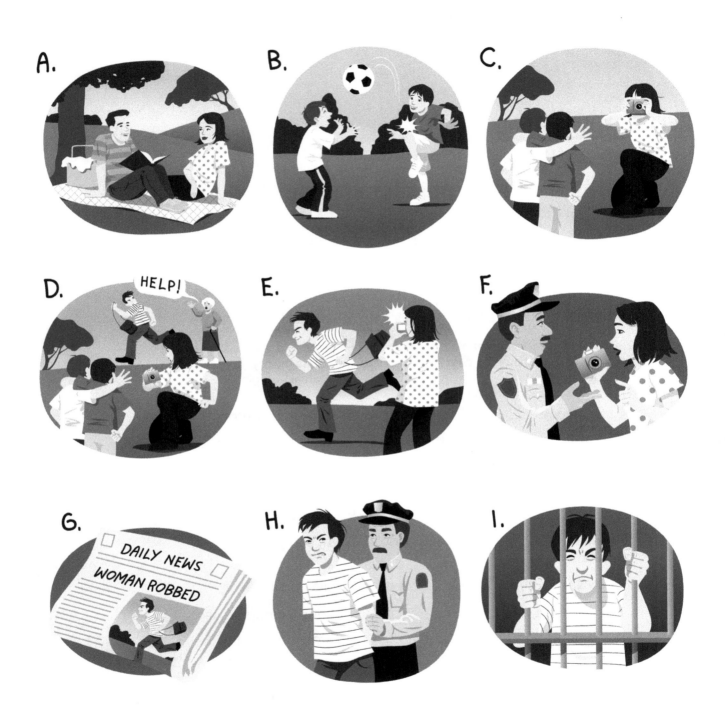

A.

B.

C.

D.

HELP!

E.

F.

G.

DAILY NEWS

WOMAN ROBBED

H.

I.

LISTENING 1: STORY

Listening Note
Retelling a story helps you to remember the information. It shows you what information you need to listen to more carefully.

(A) First Listening   Look at the pictures and listen to the story about
a robbery. After you listen, sit with a partner and retell the
information you remember about the story.

CD 4; Track 1

(B) Listen and Choose   Read the statements below, then listen to the
story again. Put a check in front of the information you know
about the robber.

CD 4; Track 1

_____ 1. He was sitting under a tree.

_____ 2. He took Sally's camera.

_____ 3. He took a woman's purse.

_____ 4. He ran away.

_____ 5. He took a picture of Sally.

_____ 6. His picture was in the newspaper.

_____ 7. He's now in jail.

(C) Match   Listen to the sentences and write the letter of the
correct picture.

CD 4; Track 2

1. _____   4. _____   7. _____

2. _____   5. _____   8. _____

3. _____   6. _____   9. _____

(D) Listen and Decide   You will hear a sentence from the story. Decide
what happened next. Circle the correct answer.

CD 4; Track 3

1. a. They talked and read.   b. Sally focused her camera.
2. a. She took out her camera.   b. She thought fast.
3. a. The police came.   b. She looked up.
4. a. She heard a scream.   b. She took three pictures
                                        of him.
5. a. She gave them her camera.   b. They arrested the man.
6. a. The photo was in the   b. The police went to
      newspaper.   his house.
7. a. They knew his address.   b. They arrested him.

(E) What do you think?   Discuss the questions with your class.

1. How did the police learn the man's name and address?
2. Why is this story called *Fast Thinking*?

STRUCTURE AND PRONUNCIATION

Ⓐ Past Tense   Complete the sentences. Use the past tense of the verbs in the box.

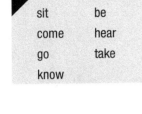

think   read
sit   be
come   hear
go   take
know

1. Sally and Jim _____ under a tree.

2. They _____ their books under a tree.

3. She _____ a woman scream.

4. Sally _____ fast.

5. She _____ three pictures of the man.

6. The police _____ in a few minutes.

7. A photograph of the man _____ in the newspaper.

8. In a few hours, the police _____ his name.

9. The police _____ to the man's house.

Ⓑ Dictation   Listen and copy the sentences you hear.

CD 4; Track 4

1. _____

2. _____

3. _____

4. _____

5. _____

6. _____

Ⓒ Tense Contrast   Listen to the sentences. Decide the tense of the verb. Circle *present*, *past*, or *future*.

CD 4; Track 5

1. present   past   future

2. present   past   future

3. present   past   future

4. present   past   future

5. present   past   future

6. present   past   future

7. present   past   future

8. present   past   future

9. present   past   future

10. present   past   future

LISTENING 2: CONVERSATIONS

Ⓐ Which One? Today, the police arrested John at his apartment. The neighbors are talking about the event. Which neighbors have a newspaper? Put a check after those conversations.

CONVERSATION 1 _____   CONVERSATION 3 _____

CONVERSATION 2 _____   CONVERSATION 4 _____

Ⓑ Listen for Expression In each conversation there is an expression of surprise. Listen to the conversations again and write the letter(s) of the expression(s) you hear.

Conversation   *Expression*

1. _____   a. Really?

2. _____   b. You're not serious!

3. _____   c. I can't believe it!

4. _____   d. Stop!

                               e. You're kidding!

Ⓒ Statement or Question Listen to each sentence about the story. If it is a statement, put a period at the end of the sentence. If it shows surprise, put a question mark at the end.

Examples: STATEMENT: John robbed a woman.

               QUESTION: John robbed a woman?

> **Pronunciation Note**
> To show surprise, people sometimes use question intonation. If the sentence is a statement, put a period (.) at the end. If the sentence is a question, put a question mark (?) at the end.

1. John robbed a woman

2. His picture is in the newspaper

3. He stole her purse

4. John's a nice guy

5. Some woman took his picture

6. The police came here

7. They were here

8. They arrested him

9. They arrested him today

10. He's in jail

SPEAKING

A Complete the Conversation   Sit with a partner and complete the conversation about the robbery in the park. Use your imagination!

A: Did you hear about John List, the man who lives in Apartment 3B?

B: No. What did he do?

A: _____

B: Why did he do that?

A: _____

B: When did the police come here?

A: _____

B: How did they know it was John?

A: _____

B: Did John say anything to the police?

A: _____

B: What's going to happen to John?

A: _____

CD 4; Track 8

B Listen and Retell   Listen to two students talk about a robbery. Retell the story in your own words.

C Discuss   Sit in a group and talk about your own experiences. Were you ever robbed? When? Explain what happened. Your group will ask you more questions to get more information.

UNIT 14

THE ACCIDENT

BEFORE YOU LISTEN

A Discuss   Talk about the questions.

1. Were you ever in a car accident? What happened?

2. Was anyone hurt?

3. What was the damage to the cars?

B True or False   Read the statements about motor vehicle accidents in the United States. Write *T* if the statement is true or *F* if the statement is false. Then check your answers on page 82.

_____ 1. Most accidents happen less than ten miles from home.

_____ 2. Every day, there are about 17,000 accidents in the United States.

_____ 3. About 40,000 people die every year in motor vehicle accidents.

_____ 4. More accidents occur on Friday than any other day.

_____ 5. About 80 percent of all drivers wear seatbelts.

C Key Words   Talk about the new words. Then, complete the sentences.

witness	hurt	crashed	damage	intersection	fault

1. The _____ to my car was over $3,000.

2. My sister _____ her neck in the car accident.

3. The accident was his _____ . He went through a stop sign.

4. There are a lot of accidents at the _____ of Pine Street and Mountain Avenue.

5. The car went off the street and _____ into a tree.

6. The _____ saw the accident and gave the information to the police.

LISTENING 1: STORY

 Look and Point Look at the picture of the accident scene. Point to the following people, places, and things.

Broad Street	Park Avenue	intersection
traffic light	accident	witness

Listening Note
Use the street map and the cars to try to picture the accident in your mind.

CD 4; Track 9

B First Listening   Listen to the story about Kim's accident. Try to picture the location of the cars and how the accident happened. Tell the class any information you remember about the accident.

CD 4; Track 9

C Mark the Picture   Listen to the story of this car accident one or more times. Mark the following items on the diagram:

Put a **1** to mark Kim's car.

Put a **2** to mark the other driver's car.

Put an **W** to mark the location of the witness at the time of the accident.

D True or False   Read the statements about the accident. If the statement is true, circle *T*. If the statement is false, circle *F*.

1. The accident happened in the morning.	T	F
2. Kim was driving to work.	T	F
3. The driver of the sports car was at fault.	T	F
4. The sports car went through the red light.	T	F
5. Kim drove her car home.	T	F

CD 4; Track 9

E Order of Speakers   Listen to the story again. When the police officer arrived, he spoke to three people. Decide who he spoke to first, second, and third. Write *1st, 2nd,* or *3rd* in the box under each picture.

Witness   Driver of the sports car   Kim

F What do you think?   Discuss the questions.

1. Why did this man lie about the accident?

2. What do you think will happen to the driver of the sports car?

3. Why is it important to call the police when you have an accident?

STRUCTURE AND PRONUNCIATION

Ⓐ Past Tense   Complete the sentences. Use the past tense of the verbs in the box.

drive   explain
crash   walk
arrive   go
see   say
have

1. Kim _____**had**_____ the green light.

2. She _____ into the intersection.

3. A small sports car _____ through the red light.

4. It _____ into the side of Kim's car.

5. The police _____ in five minutes.

6. Kim _____ the accident to the police officer.

7. The other driver _____ the accident was Kim's fault.

8. A man _____ over to the officer.

9. He _____ the accident happen.

Ⓑ Dictation   Listen and copy the sentences you hear.

CD 4; Track 10

1. _____

2. _____

3. _____

4. _____

5. _____

Ⓒ Listen for Stress   Underline the stressed word in each sentence.

CD 4; Track 11

Pronunciation Note

In English, we stress the most important words in a sentence. These words are said louder and longer.

1. Her story is correct.

2. This man went through the red light.

3. She had the green light.

4. He had the red light.

5. I had the green light.

6. You had the red light.

7. He said the accident was Kim's fault.

8. Kim was driving carefully.

9. The other driver lied.

10. The accident was his fault.

▶ **ANSWER KEY PAGE 79, EXERCISE B**

1. T   2. T   3. T   4. F (More accidents occur on Saturday)   5. T

Source: National Highway Traffic Safety Administration

LISTENING 2: CONVERSATIONS

A Match Officer Clark made out reports on two accidents yesterday. Listen to these conversations between Officer Clark and the drivers. After each conversation, write the number of the correct driver.

CONVERSATION 1: Driver _____   CONVERSATION 3: Driver _____

CONVERSATION 2: Driver _____   CONVERSATION 4: Driver _____

B Discuss Listen to the conversations again and discuss the questions.

1. Conversations 1 and 2:
   Do the drivers agree about all the facts in this accident?
   Who is at fault in this accident?

2. Conversations 3 and 4:
   Do the drivers agree about how the accident happened?
   Who is at fault in this accident?

C Repeating or Questioning You will hear eight short conversations between a driver and a police officer. Listen to the examples, then, circle *repeating* or *questioning*.

In the first example, the officer is repeating the information.

> DRIVER: I was driving along First Street.
>
> OFFICER: You were driving along First Street.

In the second example, the officer is questioning the information. The intonation is the same as for a question.

> DRIVER: I was driving along First Street.
>
> OFFICER: You were driving along First Street?

1. repeating   questioning   5. repeating   questioning

2. repeating   questioning   6. repeating   questioning

3. repeating   questioning   7. repeating   questioning

4. repeating   questioning   8. repeating   questioning

SPEAKING

A Complete the Conversation   The next day, Kim told her coworkers about her accident. Imagine that you are Kim. Sit with a partner and complete the conversation.

1: Where was the accident?

2: On Broad Street.

1: What happened?

2: _____

1: Did you have the green light?

2: _____

1: Was anyone hurt?

2: _____

1: How's your car?

2: _____

1: Were there any witnesses?

2: _____

CD 4; Track 14

B Listen and Answer   Read the questions below, then, listen to two students talk about an accident. Circle the questions you can answer. Listen again and answer the questions.

1. Where did the accident happen?

2. What time did the accident happen?

3. What were the weather conditions?

4. How fast was she going?

5. Who else was in the car?

6. Was anyone hurt?

7. What was the damage to her car?

8. Did the police/ambulance come?

9. Whose fault was the accident?

C Discuss   Sit in a small group and talk about an accident that you had, you saw, or that you know about. The other students in your group can ask you questions.

MY NEIGHBOR

BEFORE YOU LISTEN

Ⓐ Discuss   Talk about the questions.

1. Do you know your neighbors?
2. Do the people in your neighborhood ever help each other?

Ⓑ Complete   Look at the picture and complete the sentences.

Verb	Person	Crime
mug	mugger	mugging

1. _____ is a crime.
2. These men are _____.
3. They _____ an older man.
4. The police are looking for the _____.

Ⓒ Key Words   Talk about the new words. Then, complete the sentences.

neighborhood	alley	acted like
beat	shouted	passed

1. When a man tried to steal her car, the woman _____ for help.
2. The thief _____ the store owner, then stole the money.
3. The _____ between the buildings is dark and dirty.
4. I _____ my teacher when I was walking down the hall.
5. My _____ is noisy and busy.
6. I saw my friend yesterday, but she _____ she didn't know me.

LISTENING 1: STORY

Listening Note

At times, you already know some information about an event, but you don't know all of the details. To help direct your listening, ask yourself, "What do I already know about the story?" and "What questions do I have?"

A Ask Questions Look at the pictures below. You can already guess some of the information you will hear. What other information do you need to understand the story? Write three questions about the event.

B First Listening Look at the pictures and listen to this story about a mugging. After you listen, tell the class any information you remember about the story. Did you hear the answers to any of your questions?

CD 4; Track 15

C Listen and Write the Letter Listen and write the letter of the correct picture.

CD 4; Track 16

1. _____   4. _____   7. _____

2. _____   5. _____   8. _____

3. _____   6. _____   9 _____

D Listen and Choose In this story, the speaker tells about the three men who saw him in the alley. Read these sentences, then listen to the story again. Which man is the speaker talking about? Write 1st (the first man), 2nd (the second man), or 3rd (the third man).

CD 4; Track 15

_____ 1. He went to the same church.

_____ 2. He dressed differently.

_____ 3. He called the police.

_____ 4. He said, "I'll be right back."

_____ 5. He felt sorry for me.

_____ 6. He acted like he didn't see me.

_____ 7. He was from my neighborhood.

_____ 8. He stayed with me.

E Comprehension Questions Listen and circle the correct answer.

CD 4; Track 17

1. a. to work
   b. to church
   c. to visit a friend

2. a. in the morning
   b. in the evening
   c. at night

3. a. his coat and money
   b. They mugged him.
   c. in an alley

4. a. on the street
   b. in an alley
   c. in the church

5. a. a few minutes
   b. an hour
   c. all day

6. a. the first man
   b. the second man
   c. the third man

F What do you think? Discuss the questions with your class.

1. Why didn't the first two men help this man?

2. At the end of the story, does the man know the name of the person who helped him?

3. According to the speaker, who is a real neighbor?

STRUCTURE AND PRONUNCIATION

A **Past Tense**   You will hear two verbs. If they are the same, circle *same*. If they are different, circle *different*.

CD 4; Track 18

1. same   different   6. same   different
2. same   different   7. same   different
3. same   different   8. same   different
4. same   different   9. same   different
5. same   different   10. same   different

B **-ed Endings**   Listen to the pronunciation of these verbs. Write the number of syllables you hear. Then, practice saying the past tense of these verbs with a partner.

CD 4; Track 19

> 👂 **Listening Note**
>
> When a verb ends in *t* or *d*, the ed ending is a new syllable.
> With all other verbs, do not add a syllable.

1. waited   **2**   6. died   ____
2. called   **1**   7. passed   ____
3. stopped   ____   8. helped   ____
4. acted   ____   9. shouted   ____
5. stayed   ____   10. dressed   ____

C **Dictation**   Listen and copy the sentences you hear.

CD 4; Track 20

1. _____
2. _____
3. _____
4. _____
5. _____
6. _____

LISTENING 2: CONVERSATIONS

 A Match Listen to the conversations between a police dispatcher and four different callers. Write the number of each conversation on the correct picture.

 B Same or Different Read each sentence. Then listen to the sentence. Decide if the meaning of the two sentences is the same or different. Circle same or different.

1. My car isn't here.   same   different

2. Come here fast.   same   different

3. Stay on the line.   same   different

4. She wants to get into the car.   same   different

5. Someone is getting into my   same   different
   neighbor's house.

6. They are shouting out the window   same   different
   to a friend.

7. There's a problem in the apartment   same   different
   downstairs.

C What do you think? Discuss the questions with your class.

1. Which situation is the most serious?

2. Would you call the police in each of these situations?

3. Would you try to help in any of these situations?

SPEAKING

CD 4; Track 23

A The Robbery   You are a clerk in a jewelry store. A few minutes ago a woman came into the store and asked to look at some expensive necklaces. Suddenly, she pulled out a gun, took the jewelry, and asked for the money in the cash register. Now, a police officer is asking you questions. Circle the correct answer.

1. a. She had a gun.
   b. She left very fast.
   c. She took about $5,000 in jewelry and cash.

2. a. About 15 minutes ago.
   b. For about five minutes.
   c. About $2,000 in cash.

3. a. No, no one was with her.
   b. No, no one else was in the store.
   c. No, she wasn't.

4. a. She was a tall, heavy woman with blond hair.
   b. She had a big pocketbook.
   c. She was nervous.

5. a. A small, black gun.
   b. She put everything in her pocketbook.
   c. A red dress.

6. a. Yes, it is.
   b. Yes, she was.
   c. Yes, she did.

7. a. No, no one else was in the store.
   b. Don't move!
   c. She stayed here about five minutes.

8. a. I was very surprised.
   b. She ran up the street.
   c. She was wearing big gold earrings.

9. a. No, she didn't get into a car.
   b. She ran up Main Street.
   c. She said, "Thank you" when she left the store.

B An Emergency Call   You are at home when you hear a woman screaming. You look out your window and see the scene below. Sit with a partner and practice making an emergency call to the police. Act out your conversation in front of the class.

C Write the Conversation   You called the police and reported the crime. Now, the police are interviewing you. They need information about the mugger. Sit with a partner and write an interview. One of you is the witness; the other is the police officer.

> ### HELPFUL LANGUAGE
> Where were you?
>
> What time was it?
>
> Please describe the mugger.
>
> How old was he?
>
> What was he wearing?
>
> Do you remember anything special about him?
>
> Can you describe the car?
>
> Did you see any part of the license?
>
> Which way did he go?

AUDIOSCRIPTS

UNIT 1: Back in School

Listening 1 (Page 3)

Story

It's September 10th, the second week of school. This is the Dallas Adult School. There are classes for math, reading, and computers. And there are classes for English.

My class is in room 201. I'm in beginning English, the first class. This is my fourth year in the United States, but I don't speak English. I only know some easy words, like "girl" and "car" and "house."

I'm a little nervous about school. Maybe I'm too old to learn English. I'm 40 years old. English is difficult for me.

But, I want to learn English very much. This year my three children are in school. They all speak English. Sometimes, they speak English to each other, and I don't understand them. I want to talk to their friends and I want to talk to their teachers.

There are ten students in our class from many different countries. Four students are like me; they're from Mexico. Sonia, my sister, is in my class. There are three students from Vietnam, one from India, one from Haiti, and one from Poland.

Our teacher is Ms. Lang. She's young, only about 23 or 24. But she's a good teacher. I understand her because she speaks slowly. We all speak English in class.

Our class is three hours every day. It's from 9:00 to 12:00. There's a break at 10:30. We all go to the cafeteria and talk and drink coffee.

I like school. It's not easy and we have a lot of homework. But I'm happy to be back in school.

C. True or False   Listen to these statements. Circle *T* if the statement is true or *F* if the statement is false.

1. This is the first day of school.
2. Ana knows a lot of words in English.
3. Ana is nervous about school.
4. English is easy for her.
5. Her children speak English.
6. The class is small.
7. All of the students are from Mexico.
8. The teacher is a young man.
9. At the break, the students do their homework.

Structure and Pronunciation (Page 4)

A. Singular or Plural   Listen and circle the word you hear. Is the word singular or plural?

1. classes	6. schools
2. rooms	7. student
3. word	8. hour
4. friends	9. days
5. teacher	10. weeks

B. Dictation   Listen and write the words you hear.

1. schools	6. words
2. year	7. rooms
3. books	8. page
4. teacher	9. students
5. day	10. job

Listening 2 (Page 5)

Announcement 1:

We are going to use the book *Beginning English* in this class. You need to buy this book. *Beginning English* is $20. You can buy it any day this week in the main office.

Announcement 2:

Class is from 9:00 to 12:00. We have a 15 minute break at 10:30. The break is from 10:30 to 10:45. You can sit in class, or walk around, or go to the cafeteria. But, please, be back in class on time.

Announcement 3:

If you park in the school parking lot, you need a parking sticker. A sticker is $5.00. Put the sticker on the window of your car. Then, you can park in the school parking lot. You can get your sticker in the main office.

Announcement 4:

Please do not bring your children to class for any reason. If your child is sick, do not bring him to class. If your child has a day off from school, please find a baby-sitter or ask a friend to watch the child.

Announcement 5:

English class is on Monday, Wednesday, and Friday mornings. There are other classes on Tuesday and Thursday. Math and computers are on Tuesday and Thursday. They're at the same time, from 9:00 to 11:00. If you want to register for math or computers, go to the main office.

Announcement 6:

If you are absent, call the main office. Give your name to the secretary and say you are in English 1. Tell the secretary that you cannot come to class. The secretary will give me the information.

C. Listen and Complete   The students are asking Ms. Lang to repeat some information. Listen and complete these conversations.

1. MS. LANG: You can buy the book in the main office.
   STUDENT: Excuse me. Where?
2. MS. LANG: The book is $20.
   STUDENT: Excuse me. How much?
3. MS. LANG: Class begins at 9:00.
   STUDENT: Excuse me. What time?
4. MS. LANG: The break is at 10:30.
   STUDENT: Excuse me. What time?
5. MS. LANG: The break is 15 minutes.
   STUDENT: Excuse me. How long?
6. MS. LANG: You can get the sticker in the main office.
   STUDENT: Excuse me. Where?

Speaking (Page 6)

A. Introductions   Listen to these students introduce themselves. What expressions do they use?

1. **A:** Hi. I'm Ana. I'm in your English class.
   B: Hi, Ana. I'm Samir.
   A: Nice to meet you.
   B: Nice to meet you, too.
2. **A:** Hi. My name is Sabrina. What's your name?
   B: My name is Vinh.
   A: Vinh? How do you spell that?
   B: V-I-N-H.

UNIT 2: Ali

Listening 1 (Page 9)

Story

My name is Ali. I'm from Egypt. I'm a student at Oakdale University. I study English, math, and computers. I live with my aunt and uncle. We live in a small apartment building on the second floor. There are four families in this building.

There's a family of four living under us, the Ramirez family. They're from Mexico. Carlos Ramirez is a mail carrier. His wife, Maria Ramirez is a school bus driver. They have two sons—they're twins, Manuel and Michael. They're ten years old and in the fourth grade.

In the apartment next to us, there's a single man. He's from India. Mr. Patel is old; I think he's about 68 years old. He's a retired teacher. He has a lot of relatives – his three brothers, his two sisters, and lots of nieces and nephews, and they visit him a lot.

In the fourth apartment, the apartment under Mr. Patel, there's a young couple from Vietnam, Dahn and Kim Tran. Dahn's a student at Oakdale University, like me. We're in the same English class and we walk to school together. Kim is an x-ray technician.

All the people in my apartment building are friendly. They're good neighbors.

C. Listen for Numbers   Look at the picture and answer these questions with the correct number.

1. How many people live in Ali's apartment?
2. How many apartments are there in this building?
3. How many children do Mr. and Mrs. Ramirez have?
4. How old are the boys?
5. How many people live in the apartment next to Ali?
6. How old is Mr. Patel?
7. How many people live on the first floor?
8. How many people live in this apartment building?

D. Comprehension Questions   Listen and circle the correct answer.

1. Where is Ali from?
2. Who does he live with?
3. Where does the Ramirez family live?
4. Is Mr. Ramirez a mail carrier or a school bus driver?
5. Where is Mr. Patel from?
6. Is he married?
7. Are Ali and Dahn in the same English class?
8. Who is a student?

Structure and Pronunciation (Page 10)

B. Dictation   Listen and write the sentences you hear.

1. Ali is from Egypt.
2. Ali and Dahn are students.
3. They are in the same English class.
4. Dahn is married.
5. There are four families in the apartment building.
6. All the people are friendly.

C. Pronunciation   Repeat the expressions that people use to say *Hello* and *Good-bye*. See page 10 for *Hello* and *Goodbye* chart.

Listening 2 (Page 11)

Conversations

Conversation 1:

Mr. Patel: Hello, Maria.
Maria: Hi, Mr. Patel. How's everything?
Mr. Patel: Very well, thank you. I'm waiting for my brother.
Maria: Your older brother?
Mr. Patel: Yes, he's coming this morning. How're the boys?
Maria: They're good. It's raining so hard . . . I'm driving them to school.
Mr. Patel: Drive carefully.
Maria: Thanks. Have a good day.

Conversation 2:

Kim: Hi, Carlos.
Carlos: Hi, Kim.
Kim: It's not a good day for you. It's raining really hard.
Carlos: Yeah, it's going to be a long day.
Kim: Well, take care.
Carlos: You, too.

Conversation 3:

> **Mrs. Meng:** Hello, Ali.
> **Ali:** Good morning, Mrs. Meng.
> **Mrs. Meng:** What are you studying?
> **Ali:** Math. I have a math test at 9:00.
> **Mrs. Meng:** Good luck.
> **Ali:** Thank you.
> **Mrs. Meng:** I'll see you in class later.
> **Ali:** Yes. See you later.

C. Listen and Choose Listen and circle the best response.

1. How's everything?
2. How are you?
3. So long.
4. Have a nice day.
5. Hello.
6. Good afternoon.
7. Take care.
8. Good-bye.

UNIT 3: City or Country

Listening 1 (Pages 14-15)

Story

Gloria is a student in nursing school. She's going to graduate next month. She has two job offers. One is in a city hospital, the other is in a country hospital.

The hospital in the city is large; it's a 600-bed hospital. It's a cancer hospital. It gives excellent care to its patients. It's in a big city, near museums, theaters, and restaurants. The salary is high, $65,000 a year. But apartment rents are high, too.

The hospital in the country is small; it's a 50-bed hospital. It's a general hospital. It takes care of all kinds of patients. It's in a beautiful area, near lakes, rivers, and mountains. The salary is average, $50,000 a year. But apartment rents are low.

Gloria likes the city and the country. She doesn't know which hospital to choose.

C. Listen and Write the Letter Listen to the sentences. Write the letter of the correct picture.

1. The salary is average.
2. Apartment rents are low.
3. The salary is high.
4. This hospital takes care of all kinds of patients.
5. It's near museums, theaters, and restaurants.
6. Apartment rents are high.
7. It's near lakes, rivers, and mountains.
8. This hospital only takes care of cancer patients.
9. Gloria is a student in nursing school

D. Comprehension Questions Listen and circle the correct answer.

1. What is Gloria?
2. Where is the cancer hospital?
3. What kind of hospital is the country hospital?
4. What's the salary at the country hospital?
5. Which job offer will Gloria take?

Structure and Pronunciation (Page 16)

B. Dictation Listen and copy the sentences you hear.

1. The hospital in the city is large.
2. There are 600 beds in the hospital.
3. The salary in the city is high.
4. The hospital in the country is small.
5. It is a general hospital.

C. Syllables The first time you listen, write the number of syllables in each word. The second time you listen, mark the stressed syllable. The stressed syllable is longer and louder than the other syllables.

1. hospital	7. excellent	13. museum
2. school	8. area	14. city
3. apartment	9. cancer	15. country
4. mountains	10. patient	16. offer
5. student	11. job	17. nursing
6. care	12. salary	18. restaurant

D. Listen for Stress Listen and repeat the sentences. Put stress on the correct syllables.

1. Gloria is a student in nursing school.
2. She has two job offers.
3. One hospital is in the city.
4. It's near restaurants, theaters, and museums.
5. It's a cancer hospital.
6. It gives excellent care to its patients.

Listening 2 (Page 17)

Conversations

Conversation 1:

> GLORIA: I looked at a lot of apartments.
> FATHER: What's the rent in the city?
> GLORIA: A small, one-bedroom is about $1200.
> FATHER: And in the country?
> GLORIA: A large, one-bedroom is about $500.

Conversation 2:

> FATHER: What about a car?
> GLORIA: Well, I don't need a car in the city.
> FATHER: Right. You can walk or take the bus.
> GLORIA: But in the country, I need a car.
> FATHER: A car is about $22,000. And then you'll need insurance and gas.

Conversation 3:

> FATHER: What are the hours at City Hospital?
> GLORIA: They want me to work the night shift, from 11:00 to 7:00 a.m.
> FATHER: And at General Hospital?
> GLORIA: They need nurses on all shifts. I can work day, or evening, or night.
> FATHER: Which shift do you want?
> GLORIA: The day shift, from 7:00 to 3:00.

Conversation 4:

FATHER: Is the vacation the same?

GLORIA: At City Hospital, it's three weeks a year.

FATHER: And at General Hospital?

GLORIA: It's two weeks a year.

Conversation 5:

FATHER: What about the job?

GLORIA: Well, at City Hospital, I'll be a regular nurse. And I'll only work with cancer patients.

FATHER: Hmm. City Hospital is the best cancer hospital in this state.

GLORIA: And at General Hospital, they need nurses in the emergency room.

FATHER: Is that what you want? The emergency room?

GLORIA: I'm not sure. They both sound interesting.

Speaking (Page 18)

A. Interview Listen to each speaker. What is important in a job to each person?

Interview Question: What's important to you in a job?

Speaker 1: Transportation. I don't have a car, so the job has to be near my house or near the bus.

Speaker 2: For me, it's the hours. My children get home from school about 3:30, so I want to work from 7:00 to 3:00.

Speaker 3: If there are two jobs, and one pays ten dollars an hour and one pays twelve dollars an hour, I would take the one for twelve dollars an hour. Salary is the most important for me.

Speaker 4: I have a family – a wife and three children. For me, the medical benefits are more important than the salary.

UNIT 4: The Shopping Mall

Listening 1 (Page 21)

Story

B. Listen and Write the Number Listen to each shopper. Write the number of the correct picture. Listen again and explain how you decided who was speaking.

1. Mommy, please, please. Can we get a puppy? I want a puppy to play with.

2. Let me tell you about our most popular family plan. Each person in the family gets a phone. There's a limit of 5,000 minutes a month with unlimited text messaging . . .

3. Thanks, Dad. That's a great bat and glove. Can we play catch when we get home?

4. A: Let's see, ma'am . . . that's $200. Will that be cash or credit?

B: Credit. Here's my card.

5. Okay . . . Where's the security guard. He isn't watching me. He's talking on his cell phone. Good. No one's looking at me.

6. A: How do you like these sunglasses?

B: I don't know, honey. They look big on you. Try a smaller pair.

C. Listen for Information Listen to the security manager at the mall talk about the shoppers at the mall. What new information do you hear about each person?

I work the security cameras at the Riverside Mall. I'm the security manager for the mall. I watch over everything, especially the front of stores and the open areas of the mall. If there's a serious problem, I call the police. My job is really interesting and I love watching people.

There are lots of sales at the mall this weekend. Best Shoes is having its big Summer Sale. Let's see, the customer at the checkout counter is buying four, no, that's five pairs of shoes. Five pairs of shoes? She's giving her credit card to the clerk. She's going to have a big bill at the end of the month.

The woman in Sunglass Hut is trying on sunglasses. So many people try on those sunglasses. She's probably asking her husband, "How do I look in these?" The sunglasses in that store are really expensive. I buy cheap sunglasses because I'm always losing mine.

Uh-oh. See that man at the jewelry store. He looks like a businessman, but he's not. He's stealing a watch. Look at that, he's putting it in his jacket. Where's the security guard? On break?? Let me call him. Great. That security guard is always on the phone. I can't reach him . . . . And look at the thief . . . he's walking out the door. Well, I have his picture.

There's a little girl looking in the window of the pet store. And she's crying. That store has the cutest little puppies in the window. It's always the same, "Mommy, please, please. Can I have a puppy?" The little girl is asking her mother for a dog. And her mother is probably saying, "Come on. Not today. Let's get an ice cream cone."

The telephone store is busy today, as always. The telephone companies are always adding new phones and new features. That couple is looking at cell phones and talking to a clerk. Wait a minute! I know that couple. They're my neighbors, Hank and Sally Brant. They have three children. The clerk is probably telling them about different family plans. Yeah, I sometimes see people I know, but I never tell them.

There's a man walking out of the Sports Shop with his son. That little boy looks all ready for the baseball season. He's wearing a baseball hat and baseball top . . and his dad is carrying a bag with a baseball bat. Very nice . . .

D. Match Listen and write the number of the correct picture.

1. A man is stealing a watch.
2. A woman is buying five pairs of shoes.
3. A man and his son are walking out of the sports store.
4. The little girl wants a puppy.
5. A woman is trying on sunglasses.
6. A couple is talking to a clerk in the telephone store.

E. Comprehension Questions   Listen and circle the letter of the correct answer.

1. Where does the security guard work?
2. What is the man stealing?
3. Where is the child?
4. What is her mother going to buy for her?
5. Are the sunglasses in the Sunglass Hut cheap or expensive?
6. How many pairs of shoes is the woman in Best Shoes buying?
7. How many children does the couple in the cell phone store have?
8. What sport does the boy play?

Structure and Pronunciation (Page 22)

B. Dictation   Listen and write the sentences you hear.

1. The man is putting the watch in his jacket.
2. The woman is trying on sunglasses.
3. Best Shoes is having a big summer sale.
4. The couple is talking to the clerk.
5. The boy is wearing a baseball hat.

C. Contractions   Listen and repeat the contractions. Then, sit with a partner and practice saying the sentences.

1. He's putting a watch in his pocket.
2. He's walking out the door with the watch.
3. She's crying.
4. She's trying on sunglasses.
5. I'm always losing my sunglasses.
6. She's buying four pairs of shoes.
7. She's giving her credit card to the clerk.
8. He's wearing a baseball hat.

Listening 2 (Page 23)

A. Prices   Listen and write the prices you hear.

forty-nine cents

a dollar twenty-five

thirty-seven dollars

thirty-seven dollars and ninety-nine cents

a. fifty cents
b. seventy-nine cents
c. ninety-eight cents
d. a dollar seventy-five
e. a dollar thirty-nine
f. a dollar ninety-nine
g. four dollars and sixty cents
h. eleven dollars and twenty-two cents
i. fifteen dollars and ten cents
j. thirty-two dollars and twelve cents

B. How Much Is It?   Listen to each conversation and write the price.

a. **A:** How much are these sunglasses?
   B: They're on sale. They're sixteen dollars.
b. **A:** Is this ring on sale?
   B: Yes, it's twenty-nine dollars.
c. **A:** I like this sweater. How much is it?
   B: It's thirty-six dollars.
d. **A:** How much is this phone?
   B: That's our most popular model. It's on special this week for seventy-nine dollars.
e. **A:** How much are these flowers?
   B: They're five fifty.
f. **A:** How much is this pair of shoes?
   B: That pair is usually fifty dollars. We're having our summer sale and all shoes are 20 percent off, so they're forty dollars.

UNIT 5: The Bus Ride

Listening 1 (Page 27)
Story

Debbie lives about five miles from school. She always drives. Today her car is at the service center for new brakes, so she's taking the bus. At this moment, Debbie's getting on the bus and paying her fare. She's thinking about her boss. Debbie is late and when someone is late he gets angry.

Charlie is standing in back of Debbie. He's holding a five dollar bill. He's going to have a problem.

The bus is crowded and noisy. There's no place to sit and some people are standing. Mrs. Wu got on the bus before Debbie. She's holding onto a pole and using her cane. She's looking for a seat. Michael is getting up and offering Mrs. Wu his seat. She's smiling and thanking him.

Kevin is sitting on the bus with his seeing-eye dog, Jet. Jet is lying quietly next to Kevin's seat. Kevin is blind, but Jet gets him to and from work with no problems. Kevin is trying to listen to the bus driver because he always calls out the names of the bus stops. Kevin can't hear him because the bus is so loud.

Diego is sitting in the back of the bus reading his newspaper. Gina is sitting next to him. She's stealing his wallet!

Finally, the bus is moving. Debbie doesn't want to take the bus again this afternoon. At school, she's going to ask her friend for a ride home.

C. Who Questions   Answer the *Who* questions about the story. Write the name of the correct person.

1. Who is looking for a seat?
2. Who is reading the newspaper?
3. Who is holding a five dollar bill?
4. Who is trying to listen to the names of the stops?
5. Who is offering Mrs. Wu his seat?
6. Who is stealing Diego's wallet?

D. Comprehension Questions Listen and circle the correct answer.

1. Why is Debbie taking the bus?
2. How much is the bus fare?
3. Is Debbie going to sit or stand on the bus?
4. What is Debbie thinking about?
5. Why is Charlie going to have a problem?
6. Why is Kevin listening carefully?
7. How is Debbie going to get home?

Structure and Pronunciation (Page 28)

B. Dictation Listen and write the sentences you hear.

1. Debbie is taking the bus to school.
2. Charlie is getting on the bus.
3. Kevin is sitting on the bus.
4. His dog is lying next to him.
5. He's listening to the bus driver.

C. His, Her, Him Listen and complete the sentences with *his, her,* or *him*. Listen again and repeat the sentences. Then, sit with a partner and practice saying the sentences.

1. Debbie is thinking about her boss.
2. She's using her cane.
3. He's offering his seat to Mrs. Wu.
4. She's stealing his wallet.
5. Kevin is on the bus with his seeing-eye dog.
6. Jet gets him to and from work.
7. He can't hear him.
8. She's going to ask her friend for a ride.

Listening 2 (Page 29)

Conversation

Conversation 1:

WOMAN 1: Excuse me. There's no smoking on this bus.
WOMAN 2: No smoking?
WOMAN 1: That's right. See the sign?
WOMAN 2: That's crazy. I can't smoke anywhere.
WOMAN 1: Well, you can't smoke on this bus.

Conversation 2:

MAN: How much is the fare?
DRIVER: Two dollars.
MAN: Here's $5.00.
DRIVER: Sorry, sir. Exact change only.
MAN: But I don't have exact change.
DRIVER: Sorry. There's nothing I can do.

Conversation 3:

MAN: Hey, my wallet! Where's my wallet?
DRIVER: Are you sure you had your wallet?
MAN: Of course. I had it when I paid my fare. Someone on this bus took my wallet.
DRIVER: Maybe you dropped it?
MAN: No, I put it in my pocket after I paid you.

Conversation 4:

BOY: Ma'am. Here, take my seat.
WOMAN: Oh. Thank you so much. You are very polite.
BOY: That's OK.

Conversation 5:

BOY: Sir, how do you cross the street?
MAN: Jet helps me. When he sees that the cars are stopping and that people are crossing, he walks into the street. And when the cars are moving, he doesn't cross.
BOY: Wow, he's really a smart dog.
MAN: Yes, he is.

Conversation 6:

WOMAN 1: I had to take the bus to school today.
WOMAN 2: Where's your car?
WOMAN 1: At the service center. It needs new brakes.
WOMAN 2: Look, I leave about 4:00. Do you need a ride?
WOMAN 1: I'd love a ride.
WOMAN 2: Okay. I'll meet you at the library at 4:00.
WOMAN 1: Great! At the library at 4:00. Thanks.

B. Listen for Information Listen to each conversation. Complete with the correct place and time.

1. A: I'll meet you at the library at 4:00.
   B: At the library at 4:00?
   A: Yes.
2. A: I'll see you in the cafeteria at 2:00.
   B: In the cafeteria at 2:00?
   A: Uh-huh.
3. A: I'll pick you up at the bus stop at 8:00.
   B: At the bus stop at 9:00?
   A: No, at 8:00. And don't be late.
4. A: I'll see you by the front door at 1:30.
   B: Okay, the front door at 1:30.
   A: Right.
5. A: I'll meet you in Room 24 at 10:00.
   B: In Room 210 at 10:00?
   A: No, in Room 24 at 10:00.
   B: I got it. Room 24, 10:00.
6. A: I'll be at your house at 7:30.
   B: See you at 7:30.
7. A: I'll pick you up on the corner at 6:30.
   B: What corner?
   A: The corner of Front Street and Bay Street.
   B: I'll be there at 6:00.
   A: Not 6:00, 6:30.
   B: Okay.

Speaking (Page 30)

B. Listen for Information Listen to each speaker talk about getting to school. Complete the information and write one sentence about each person.

Speaker 1: I take the bus. Not a school bus, the city bus. Traffic is really heavy in the morning, so it takes about 40 minutes.

Speaker 2: I walk. I live in the city and I don't have a car, so I walk everywhere. The school is close to my house, only about five blocks. It takes me 10 minutes. Almost all the students at the school walk or take the bus because the school doesn't have any parking for the students.

Speaker 3: I drive to school. I need to take my car because after school, I go to work. It takes me about 20 minutes to get to school.

Speaker 4: My father drives me to school every day. He passes the school on his way to work, so he drops me off at school. It takes about 15 minutes to get to school from my house.

UNIT 6: The Airport

Listening 1 (Page 33)

Telephone Calls

Ladies and gentlemen, due to the heavy rain and strong wind, all flights into and out of the airport are delayed. Check the arrival and departure monitors for information about your flights. We are sorry for any inconvenience this may cause.

Samip

Hi, Mom . . . I'm at the airport . . . ahh . . . All flights are delayed. I think my flight is going to be cancelled. It's raining *really* hard . . . ahh . . .The weather forecast? It's for rain all day. I know . . I know. . . it's Bobby's wedding. Mom, there's nothing the airlines can do. The weather's terrible. Mom, don't worry . . . I'm going to get there on time. . . I'm standing at the car rental counter right now. I'm renting a car. . . ahh . . . Yeah, they have a car and I'm signing the papers. I know . . . it's 600 miles. I'm going to drive all night. Mom, it's my brother's wedding. I'm going to be there.

Sarah

Hi, hon. I'm still at the airport. I'm looking at the departure monitor and nothing is moving. No planes are boarding. . . . I'm okay. I'm sitting at the gate . . . reading the newspaper . . . I don't know. Maybe in an hour or two . . . Yeah, Dad's much better. He's out of the hospital and he has a doctor's appointment next week . . . Uh, huh. Uh, huh. You're right. Flying is no fun . . . Okay, I will. I'll get something to eat. . . . Uh, huh. I miss you too. I hope I get home today.

Jack

Jenny, I'm in the security line. Everything is so different from the last time . . . I know, I haven't been on a plane for ten years. But, . . this is crazy. I understand . . . they're checking bags . . people are taking off their jackets. But, their shoes? People are taking off their shoes? . . .Yes, I have my ticket. I have my driver's license. I'm not flying again. Next time I visit you and the grandchildren, I'm taking the train.

Gloria

Hi, Cindy, Gloria here. Yes, it's a mess. I'm sitting in a restaurant at the airport, but the weather is terrible. Nothing is taking off. I'm looking at my computer. The meeting in Houston is at 3:00, but, I'm not going to make it. I need you to call and change the meeting for tomorrow. . . . . And the reports? . . . Good . . . Good. So you're sending them out now. Good. Okay. I'll call again later.

Carly

Hi, Dad. Dad, I'm *still* on the plane, but the plane is just sitting here . . on the runway. Dad, it's been *three hours*. . . No, don't worry, I'm okay, but some of the passengers are upset and one kid is crying . . . Dad, don't worry. I have my cell phone and I'm talking to all my friends . . . And I have my computer with me. . . . No, don't wait at the airport for me. I'll call you when the plane arrives. Yup, see you later, Dad. . . .Don't worry . . It's all good.

Structure and Pronunciation (Page 34)

B. Dictation Listen and copy the sentences you hear.

1. Nothing is moving.
2. I'm renting a car.
3. I'm sitting at the gate.
4. They're checking bags.
5. I'm looking at my computer.

C. Expressions

> When people are speaking, they use expressions such as *ah, uh-huh, okay, I know, yeah,* and *You're right* to show that they are listening or to agree with the speaker .

Complete the sentences with the expressions you hear.

1. I'm renting a car . . ah . . . yes, they have a car.
2. I know . . I know . . ., it's Bobby's wedding.
3. Uh-huh. You're right. Flying is no fun.
4. Okay, I will. I'll get something to eat.
5. And the reports? . . Good . . . Good. So you're sending them out now. Good. Okay.

Listening 2 (Page 35)

Airport Announcements

Announcement 1:

Attention, please. Mr. Julio Vargas, please report to Gate 71. Paging Mr. Julio Vargas. Please report to gate 71.

Announcement 2:

Good evening, ladies and gentlemen. Flight 579 to Miami is now boarding. We are boarding rows 20 to 25. Please have your boarding passes ready.

Announcement 3:

Speaker: All passengers for Flight 359 to Denver, Colorado. It is snowing in Denver and the Denver airport has been closed. Due to the bad weather, we are canceling Flight 359. Please see a ticket agent to reschedule your flight to Denver. We are sorry for any inconvenience.

Announcement 4:

Passengers on flight 222, this flight is overbooked. We are looking for two passengers to change their flights. We are offering first class seats on the next flight to Boston. That flight leaves in four hours. You will also receive a voucher for $300 to use on a future flight. Please come to the ticket counter if you can take the next flight.

Announcement 5:

Passengers on flight 449 to London, there is a gate change. The Flight is not leaving from Terminal A, Gate 25. Please go to Terminal C. Flight 449 is leaving from Terminal C, Gate 120

Announcement 6:

Ladies and gentlemen, because of the rain, Flight 688 scheduled to leave at 9:45 is delayed. The new departure time is 11:15. The new departure time for Flight 688 is 11:15. We thank you for your patience.

UNIT 7: Eduardo

Listening 1 (Pages 38-39)
Story
Conversation 1:

   F: Tomorrow's the big day.
   E: Yup, my last day at work for one month.
   F: How are you going to get to the airport?
   E: My cousin is going to drive me.
   F: So, I'm sure you're going to spend a lot of time with Yolanda.
   E: We are. It's summer in Colombia now and we're going to go to the beach. And we're going to spend time with her family and with my family. And we're going to go to her cousin's wedding together.
   F: Are you going to return alone? Or is Yolanda going to come back with you?
   E: I really don't know. We'll see.

Conversation 2:

   Y: I had such a good time today, Eduardo.
   E: Me, too. We've seen each other every day for three weeks and every day with you is special.
   Y: Oh, Eduardo, I'm so happy.
   E: What are we going to do? I have to go back next week, but I don't want to leave you.
   Y: And I don't want you to leave.
   E: I can't stay, I have a good job in the United States. I live there.
   Y: I know.
   E: I'm going to ask you something, but I don't want you to answer *Yes* or *No*. I want you to think about it and talk to your family. Yolanda, I love you.
   Y: I love you, too.
   E: . . . and I want to marry you. I want you to come to the United States with me. Yolanda, I want you to think about it and talk to your mother, and your father. Please, talk to them before you give me an answer.

Conversation 3:

   Y: Mom, I love Eduardo. He loves me. We don't know what to do.
   M: Yolanda, I knew that this was going to happen.
   Y: I thought so, too, Mom.
   M: Yolanda, it's going to be very hard.
   Y: I know, Mom.
   M: If you go, I'm going to miss you so much. All your family and friends are here.
   Y: I know.
   M: I have so many questions. What is your life going to be like? You don't know English. Where are you going to work? When are we going to see you again?
   Y: Yes, Mom, I have to learn English. I don't know about my life.
   M: And what are you going to do if you have a baby? I won't be able to help you!
   Y: I know, Mom.
   M: And your children, they're going to be Americans, not Colombians.
   Y: I know, Mom. I'm worried . . but I love Eduardo.

Conversation 4:

   Y: Dad, I love Eduardo and he loves me.
   F: I know. I can see it in your eyes and your smile.
   Y: Dad, Eduardo asked me to marry him. But he wants me to talk to mom and to talk to you. He says life in the United States is hard at first.
   F: What does your heart say?
   Y: It says that I love him and I want to be with him.
   F: Yolanda, follow your heart. I'm going to miss you, but I know you love him and he's a very good man.
   Y: Thank you, Dad.

D. Listen and Circle Yolanda's mother is worried about her daughter leaving home. What are some of her worries? Listen and circle the things that Yolanda's mother spoke about.

   Y: Mom, I love Eduardo. He loves me. We don't know what to do.
   M: Yolanda, I knew that this was going to happen.
   Y: I thought so, too, Mom.
   M: Yolanda, it's going to be very hard.
   Y: I know, Mom.
   M: If you go, I'm going to miss you so much. All your family and friends are here.
   Y: I know.
   M: I have so many questions. What is your life going to be like? You don't know English. Where are you going to work? When are we going to see you again?
   Y: Yes, Mom, I have to learn English. I don't know about my life.
   M: And what are you going to do if you have a baby? I won't be able to help you!
   Y: I know, Mom.
   M: And your children, they're going to be Americans, not Colombians.
   Y: I know, Mom. I'm worried . . . but I love Eduardo.

Structure and Pronunciation (Page 40)

B. Dictation   Listen and write the questions you hear.

1. How are you going to get to the airport?
2. Is Yolanda going to come back with you?
3. Are you going to return alone?
4. Where are you going to work?
5. When are we going to see you again?

C. Going To   Listen and repeat the sentences. Then, sit with a partner and practice the sentences together. Refer to Exercise C on page 40 for sentences.

1. Eduardo and Yolanda are going to get married.
2. He's going to give her a ring.
3. Yolanda is going to plan the wedding.
4. Eduardo is going to return to Colombia in four months.
5. They are going to have a big wedding.
6. Eduardo is going to return to the United States with Yolanda.

Listening 2 (Page 41)

Conversations

Conversation 1:

EDUARDO:	And Yolanda, you don't speak English.
YOLANDA:	Yes, I'm worried about that. My friend told me that English is very difficult.
EDUARDO:	I'm not home a lot. I work nine or ten hours a day.
YOLANDA:	What am I going to do all day?
EDUARDO:	You'll feel lonely, too. You'll miss your family.
YOLANDA:	Eduardo, I'm not sure I can leave my family. Can you move back here?

Conversation 2:

EDUARDO:	And Yolanda, you don't speak English.
YOLANDA:	I know. I can go to school.
EDUARDO:	I'm not home a lot. I work nine or ten hours a day.
YOLANDA:	Maybe I can find a job.
EDUARDO:	You'll feel lonely, too. You'll miss your family.
YOLANDA:	Eduardo, you are going to be my family. I know it isn't going to be easy, but we can do it together.

C. Listen and Circle   Listen to each statement from Eduardo. Is Yolanda an optimist or a pessimist in each reply? Circle *optimist* or *pessimist*.

1. **A:** You have to learn English.
   B: I can go to school and learn it. I'm good at languages.
2. **A:** You'll miss your family.
   B: I can e-mail them and call them.
3. **A:** I have a car. I can teach you to drive.
   B: Drive? I'm scared that I'll have an accident.
4. **A:** All your friends are here.
   B: I'll make new friends.
5. **A:** You'll want to find a job.
   B: How can I find a job if I don't speak English?
6. **A:** It's very cold in the winter.
   B: I hate the cold. I'll stay in the house all winter.
7. **A:** I work all day.
   B: I want to find a job, too. We'll both be busy.
8. **A:** New York is a big city.
   B: There will always be things to do.

UNIT 8: The Divorce

Listening 1 (Page 45)

Story

Marsha and Tom Gibson are sitting at the kitchen table. Tom is nervous and upset. Marsha's eyes are red. She looks tired. Their two sons are eight and ten and they're sitting with them. Tony and George know that their parents are having problems. They argue all the time. They don't talk to each other anymore. Their mom and dad aren't happy together anymore. Now, their parents are telling the boys that they're going to get a divorce.

Their mother is talking first. She's telling them that she loves them and their father loves them, too. But, she and their father are having problems. They aren't going to live together as a family anymore. It has nothing to do with the boys. The boys are going to live with her. They're going to stay in the same house, go to the same school, and be with all their friends.

Now, their father is talking. He's going to leave the house this weekend. He's not going to move far away; he's going to be in the next town. Two weekends a month, the boys are going to stay with him. And, they're going to be with him one month in the summertime. He'll take his vacation then, and they'll go to the beach. The boys can call him anytime. He's going to be near. It'll be better this way.

Tony and George don't really understand what's happening. They know that their parents aren't happy. But, they want everyone to stay together.

B. Listen and Choose Listen and write the letter of the correct picture.

1. The boys can call their father anytime.
2. Tom and Marsha are going to get a divorce.
3. Two weekends a month, the boys are going to stay with their father.
4. The family is sitting at the kitchen table.
5. They're going to stay in the same house.
6. Tony and George don't really understand what's happening.
7. They'll go to the beach in the summertime.
8. Tom is going to leave the house this weekend.

C. Comprehension Questions Listen and circle the correct answer.

1. What school are the boys going to go to?
2. When is their father going to leave?
3. Where is he going to move?
4. When can the boys call their father?
5. How often will the boys see their father?
6. How do the boys feel?

Structure and Pronunciation

A. Tense Contrast Listen and decide if the statement is about right now or the future. Circle *right now* or *future*.

1. They are sitting at the kitchen table.
2. Tom and Marsha are talking to the boys.
3. Tom and Marsha are having problems.
4. They're going to get a divorce.
5. They're talking to the boys.
6. The boys are going to live with their mother.
7. They're going to see their father two weekends a month.
8. The boys are looking at their parents.
9. They're asking questions.
10. It's going to be difficult for everyone.

B. Dictation Listen and write the sentences you hear. All of the sentences are about the future time. Remember that in spoken English, *going to* sounds like *gonna*.

1. Tom and Marsha are going to get a divorce.
2. The boys are going to live with their mother.
3. They're going to go to the same school.
4. Their father is going to leave this weekend.
5. He's going to move to the next town.

C. Time Expressions Listen to the sentences. Fill in the time expression.

1. The boys are going to see their father two weekends a month.
2. They can call him anytime.
3. They're going to go on vacation one month in the summer.
4. Tom and Marsha argue all the time.
5. Tom is going to leave this weekend.
6. He's going to move in a few days.
7. The boys are going to see their father next weekend.
8. They're going to call their father on Sunday night.
9. Marsha is going to talk to a lawyer next week.
10. The boys are going to go to the same school next year.

Listening 2 (Page 47)

Conversations

Conversation 1:

WOMAN: When are you going to <u>fix</u> the shower?
MAN: Tomorrow.
WOMAN: <u>Tomorrow</u>. Everything is <u>tomorrow</u>. You <u>never</u> do <u>anything</u> around the house.
MAN: I'm tired.
WOMAN: You <u>always</u> say that. You do <u>nothing</u>. You just <u>sit</u> in front of the TV all day.

Conversation 2:

WOMAN: Larry, how much was this camera?
MAN: Four hundred dollars.
WOMAN: Four hundred dollars! We don't have four hundred dollars for a camera. How are we going to pay the rent tomorrow?
MAN: I don't know. You bought a new coat last week. That was two hundred dollars.
WOMAN: Well, I needed a coat.
MAN: And I needed a camera.

Conversation 3:

MAN: Where's Gina?
WOMAN: She's out with her friends.
MAN: Where?
WOMAN: At Lisa's house. They're watching TV and talking.
MAN: When's she going to be home?
WOMAN: At 11:00.
MAN: 11:00? 11:00 is too late for a 16-year-old.
WOMAN: 11:00 <u>isn't</u> too late for a 16-year-old.
MAN: I <u>don't</u> want her out this late.
WOMAN: This isn't late. It's <u>Saturday</u> night and she's just at another girl's house.

Conversation 4:

WOMAN: Sorry I'm late.
MAN: Late? Sue, you're an hour late!
WOMAN: Well, I met a friend and we started to talk.
MAN: You knew I needed the car.
WOMAN: You're just visiting your brother. He can wait.
MAN: I'm taking him to the dentist. I told you I needed the car at <u>11:00</u>.
WOMAN: Look, I <u>said</u> I was <u>sorry</u>.
MAN: You <u>never</u> think about <u>me</u>. It's always what <u>you</u> want.

B. Word Stress Listen and circle the word or words that are stressed.

Pronunciation Note: Stress

The most important words in a sentence are stressed. These words are the longest and loudest in the sentence.
Example: You ⟦never⟧ do ⟦anything⟧.

1. You <u>always</u> say that.
2. You do <u>nothing</u>.
3. How are we going to pay the <u>rent</u>?
4. <u>You</u> bought a new <u>coat</u>.
5. I <u>needed</u> a coat.
6. And <u>I</u> needed a <u>camera</u>.
7. 11:00 <u>isn't</u> too late for a 16-year-old.
8. I <u>don't</u> want her out this late.
9. You <u>never</u> think about <u>me</u>.
10. It's always what <u>you</u> want.

UNIT 9: My Family

Listening 1 (Pages 50-51)

Story

A: Oh, look at all the pictures you have on your desk. You have to tell me about them. Who's this with the big hat? Your mother?

B: Yes, that's my mom, . . . her name's Katrina. She's a teacher . . . she teaches first grade . . . and she lives in Mexico.

A: When do you see her?

B: In the summer. We're finished with classes here in May, so I live with Mom in June, July, and August.

A: Is this your father, with the moustache?

B: Hmm-hmm. That's Dad. My Mom and Dad are divorced. They got divorced when I was little. My Dad's name is Oscar and this is his wife, Sarah. She's my stepmother, but I call her Sarah. She's American. And she and Dad have a little girl, Ashley. So she's my stepsister. She's eight years old and in third grade.

A: Does your Dad live here in Dallas?

B: He lives in Houston and he works for a bank there. I visit him on the holidays and I sometimes drive there for a weekend.

A: Who's this? He's cute.

B: That's my brother, Antonio, but everyone calls him Tony. He's 23 and he's in the army. He was in Germany for two years and now he's in Korea. Don't get any ideas . . . he's engaged and his fiancée . . . her name is Katie . . . is from Canada.

A: Is this your sister? She looks like you.

B: Yes, that's Jenny. She has dark hair and glasses, like me. Jenny's 28 and she's the oldest. Her husband works for a company in China and they live in Beijing. They have two little boys and Jenny is pregnant again. She's hoping for a girl.

A: China! Did you ever visit her?

B: Yeah, I visited her last summer and I studied Chinese. I'm studying hotel management in college and I'm learning Chinese. I think I'd like to work in a hotel in China after I graduate.

A: You sure are an international family!

B: Yeah, we're all over the world. We keep in touch by e-mail and my sister sends pictures of the little boys all the time. And Tony is getting married this summer in Canada . . . in Toronto. I can't wait because everyone's going. We'll all be able to see each other and the new baby.

D. Active Listening Read the statements. Then, listen to the questions and match each with the correct answer or response.

1. Who's this with the big hat? Your mother?
2. When do you see her?
3. Is this your father, with the moustache?
4. Does your Dad live here in Dallas?
5. Is this your sister?
6. Did you ever visit her?
7. Who's this? He's cute.

Structure and Pronunciation (Page 52)

B. Dictation Listen and copy the sentences you hear.

1. My mother teaches first grade.
2. She lives in Mexico.
3. My father works for a bank.
4. I visit him on the holidays.
5. I sometimes drive there for a weekend.

C. Linking Listen and mark the linking sounds. Then, listen again and repeat the sentences.

Pronunciation note: Many words in English are linked, or joined, together. Put the final consonant of a word together with the next vowel.

She's‿a teacher. She lives‿in Mexico.

1. She's American
2. They have a little girl.
3. She's eight.
4. She's in third grade.
5. He lives in Houston.
6. He works in a bank.
7. He's in the army.
8. They live in Beijing.
9. We keep in touch by e-mail.
10. I'd like to work in a hotel.

Listening 2 (Page 53)

Conversations

Conversation 1:

A: Okay, Julie, I know you brought photographs with you. Let's see your granddaughter.

B: Here she is! This is Emily. We got the pictures on our e-mail last night.

A: Oh-h-h! She's beautiful! Look at that curly hair! Who do you think she looks like, your daughter or your son-in-law?

B: My daughter says she looks like Tom. She has the same eyes, the same hair.

A: And you can't wait to see her.

B: We're flying out to California on Friday.

A: How long are you taking off from work?

B: Two weeks.

Conversation 2:

A: Oh! Are these your children?

B: Yes, my sons. This is Max. He's 8. And this is Adam. He's 5.

A: Look at those smiles! What grades are they in?

B: Max is in third grade and Adam is in kindergarten.

A: Who watches the boys after school?

B: My mother-in-law lives in town and she picks them up every day after school. I get home by 5:00.

A: You are so lucky!

Conversation 3:

A: Hey, Bob, is this the family?

B: Yep, that's Kathy and the kids.

A: I thought you had two girls.

B: Yeah, two girls . . . and two boys!

A: Where are you in this photo? At the beach?

B: Yes, I took that photo on vacation last summer.

A: How old are the kids? It looks like they're all teenagers!

B: Amy and Megan are in high school They're 13 and 15. Josh is 19 and he's in college, studying computers. Dave is twenty. He's in the army.

A: All those kids! How do you do it? Girlfriends . . . boyfriends . . . cars . . . . . school . . college. I'm having trouble with one!

Speaking (Page 54)

B. Listen and Write Listen and write questions we often ask when looking at photos.

Children

1. Who's this?
2. How old is she?
3. What grade is he in?

Adults

1. Who's this?
2. Where does she live?
3. What does she do?
4. Is she married?
5. How often do you see her?

UNIT 10: The Sunset Motel

Listening 1 (Page 56-57)

Story

The Sunset Motel is a small, old motel near a busy highway. The motel is not in a city, not in a vacation area. The only people who stay at the motel are tired drivers, on their way to visit friends or family or on the way to business in another area. The Sunset Motel is not in a small town. There is a gas station on one side, and a small restaurant down the road. The motel has no pool, no restaurant, and no exercise room. The rooms are small with small televisions. There are no telephones and there is no Internet. There are only two reasons that people stay the night at the Sunset Motel – it's near the highway and it's cheap. Most people drive in at 8:00 or 9:00 at night. They leave early the next morning.

B. Write the Name Listen to the description of the hotel, the employees and the owner. Write the name of the correct person: Jack, Mabel, or Mr. Higgins.

Dan Higgins is the owner and manager of the Sunset Motel.

Mr. Higgins has two employees, a desk clerk and a housekeeper. The desk clerk is Jack Jones. Jack is friendly and helpful to all the guests. He registers guests and gives them keys to their rooms. But, Jack makes a lot of mistakes. Sometimes he gives guests the wrong key. If a guest is staying in room 12, he gives him the key for room 11. Sometimes he makes mistakes on the bills. For example, if the bill is $59, he charges $49.

The housekeeper is Mabel Morse. Mabel is not dependable. Sometimes she comes to work, but sometimes she doesn't. Work starts at 8:00 in the morning. She often comes in at 8:30 or 9:00. She cleans very well, but she sometimes forgets things. Sometimes, she forgets to vacuum a room. Sometimes she doesn't put clean towels in the bathroom. She never remembers to check the closet and people often leave a coat or their shoes in the closet.

Mr. Higgins needs more dependable workers. But, Mr. Higgins isn't easy to work for. He isn't friendly and he doesn't smile. He always complains. He complains about everyone and everything. And, Mr. Higgins is cheap, just like his motel. He pays very little. He only gives his employees the minimum wage.

C. Match Read the examples below. Then, listen to each statement. Match the statement and the example.

1. He sometimes gives guests the wrong key.
2. The motel is cheap.
3. Mabel sometimes forgets things.
4. Mabel is not dependable.
5. Jack sometimes makes mistakes on the bills.
6. Mr. Higgins pays very little.
7. Mr. Higgins isn't easy to work for.
8. People don't stay at the motel for long.

Structure and Pronunciation (Page 58)

B. Dictation   Listen and copy the sentences you hear.

1. The motel doesn't have a restaurant.
2. The rooms don't have telephones.
3. Jack makes a lot of mistakes.
4. Mr. Higgins isn't easy to work for.
5. Mabel doesn't like her job.

C. Contractions   Listen and repeat the sentences. Then, sit with a partner and read the sentences to one another. Be careful of the pronunciation of the contractions.

> Pronunciation Note: Negative contractions end in 't, for example, *isn't* and *doesn't*. These contractions have two syllables, but the final *t* is not strong.

1. The motel isn't in a city.
2. The area isn't noisy.
3. The motel isn't expensive.
4. The motel doesn't have a restaurant.
5. The owner isn't friendly.
6. He doesn't smile at people.
7. He isn't easy to work for.

Listening 2 (Page 59)

Conversations: Job Interview

Mr. H: Do you have any experience?

Carla: Yes, I was a desk clerk at Motel 7.

Mr. H: That's a big motel chain. We are independent here. How many rooms did your motel have?

Carla: We had 125 rooms.

Mr. H: Hmm. 125 rooms.

Carla: Yes. How large is your motel?

Mr. H: We have twelve rooms.

Carla: Twelve rooms. That's very small.

Carla: What computer system do you use?

Mr. H: We don't have a computer in the office. We do everything by hand.

Carla: Oh . . . you don't use a computer.

Mr. H: No, we don't need one. We use the telephone and paper.

Carla: What are the hours?

Mr. H: 1:00 to 9:00.

Carla: 1:00 to 9:00. And how long is the dinner break?

Mr. H: The dinner break? There's no dinner break.

Carla: You mean I get no time for dinner?

Mr. H: You can eat your dinner at the desk. It's very slow here.

Carla: And what days are you looking for a desk clerk?

Mr. H: We need someone from Tuesday to Sunday. Monday is your day off.

Carla: So, you need someone six days a week, eight hours a day.

Mr. H: That's right.

Carla: That's 48 hours a week. What is the pay?

Mr. H: I pay minimum wage.

Carla: Minimum wage?! What do you pay for overtime? That's eight hours extra a week.

Mr. H: There is no overtime. It's minimum wage.

Carla: Mr. Higgins, I have four years experience as a desk clerk. I'm not interested in this position.

UNIT 11: Alaska

Listening 1 (Page 63)
Story

If you have the opportunity, visit Alaska. It is one of the most interesting states in the United States.

Alaska is the largest state. It is more than twice as big as Texas. Alaska is not part of the lower 48 states. It is located far to the north. Canada borders Alaska on the east. Russia is across the Bering Strait, about 55 miles to the west. Two oceans border Alaska, the Arctic Ocean on the north and the Pacific Ocean on the south. The longest river in Alaska is the Yukon and it runs through the middle of the state. Mt. Denali is the tallest mountain in the United States.

Alaska has the smallest population of any state in the United States, only about 670,00 people. The largest city in Alaska is Anchorage and about half the people in Alaska live in this city. The capital of Alaska is Juneau. There is no major highway into Juneau. The only way into Juneau is by plane or by ship. Barrow is far to the north. In Barrow, the sun rises on May 10th and it does not set for three months. That means the sun stays out for three months, day and night. But, when the sun goes down on November 18, it does not rise again for three months. That means it is dark for three months. Barrow is also the coldest city in the United States. The temperature is below freezing more than 325 days a year. The average temperature in this city is 9 degrees, minus 13 degrees Celsius.

Alaska has many small towns with a population of 200 people or less. In Alaska, people travel long distances to work, stores, and school. Many people have small planes that can land on water, ice, or land. Some areas, especially in the north, do not have roads. In these areas, people drive on ice roads in the winter.

Oil is Alaska's largest industry. Alaska produces 7 percent of the oil used in the United States. Prudhoe Bay is the home of the oil industry. The Trans-Alaska Pipeline carries the oil 800 miles from Prudhoe Bay to Valdez. In Valdez, ships wait to take the oil to seaports in the United States.

Tourism is another important industry. Thousands of tourists visit Alaska each year. The rivers in Alaska have the best salmon fishing in the world. Many of the salmon are 40 and 50 pounds. Cruises in the Gulf of Alaska are very popular and tourists can see large glaciers, whales, birds, bears, and other wildlife, or spend the day hiking, fishing, biking, or kayaking.

The best time to visit Alaska is the summer. The temperature is cool, but not cold. Bring a sweater and a jacket. And remember your rain jacket. In some parts of Alaska, it rains several days a week in the summer.

Structure and Pronunciation (Page 64)

B. Pronunciation   Listen and repeat each superlative adjective.

1. the largest
2. the smallest
3. the best
4. the coldest
5. the biggest
6. the tallest
7. the longest
8. the most

C. Dictation   Listen and complete these sentences. Each sentence uses an adjective from exercise B. Then, listen again and repeat the sentences.

1. Alaska is the largest state.
2. The Yukon is the longest river in Alaska.
3. Mt. Denali is the tallest mountain.
4. Barrow is the coldest city in the United States.
5. Oil is Alaska's largest industry.
6. Summer is the best time to visit Alaska.

Listening 2 (Page 65)

Conversations

Conversation 1, Matt:

A: How do you like the weather in North Carolina?
B: I live in Charlotte and I like the weather here all year. Summer is my favorite season. We have a small garden and we grow tomatoes, peppers, green beans . . . lots of things. And we have strawberries and blueberries, too.

Conversation 2, Cindy:

A: How's the weather in Illinois?
B: I live in Chicago. I love the summers here because we live near Lake Michigan. On the weekends, we go to one of the beaches or to the park.

Conversation 3, Sam:

A: How do you like the weather in Colorado?
B: If you like outdoor activities, the weather here is wonderful. In the summer, it's warm, so you can walk, or ride a bike, or hike in the mountains. In the winter, it's cold and it snows a lot. That's my favorite season. I love to ski, so I really like the winter here.

Conversation 4, Lauri

A: How's the weather in New York?
B: I like the weather in New York City. We have all four seasons, and I really like the change in seasons. Uh, I guess my favorite season is spring. The winter is cold and long, but when spring comes, the days get warmer. Everything looks beautiful. The trees and flowers come out. Winter is finally over and I just feel happier.

UNIT 12: Good Health

Listening 1 (Page 69)

Story

Len just turned 50 last week. He's a successful businessman, the president of a large company. Len lives in a beautiful home with his wife and two daughters. He drives an expensive car and wears the best clothes. He has everything that money can buy, except for one thing, good health.

It happened one afternoon at the office. Len didn't feel well all that morning. He was hot and a little dizzy. He remembers the terrible pain in his chest. He remembers the faces of his wife and daughter in the emergency room. For two weeks Len was in the cardiac care unit of the hospital. Before leaving the hospital, Len got his orders from the doctor. He's trying to follow them.

First, Len has to change his diet. He has to lose fifty pounds. In the morning, he can't have his usual bacon and eggs for breakfast. And he has to drink decaffeinated coffee. For lunch, he can't order the salty french fries that he loves so much. For dinner, he has to eat fish or chicken and a vegetable. Len hates vegetables and he dreams about steak.

Second, Lens needs to exercise every day. In the morning, he has to walk one mile. In the afternoon, he has to exercise at a health club. At first, he can exercise for fifteen or twenty minutes a day. After two or three months, he will feel stronger and will be able to exercise for an hour.

Next, Len has to stop smoking. He used to smoke a pack of cigarettes every day. He can't smoke anymore.

Finally, Len also has to slow down at the office. He can't work this month; he has to stay home. When he returns to work, he can only work four hours a day. He can increase his hours each month, but he can't work more than seven hours a day. Len misses the long hours and the excitement of the office. How did this happen to him? He's only 50 years old.

C. Listen and Write the Letter   Listen to these sentences. Write the letter of the correct picture.

1. Len can't smoke.
2. Len has to slow down at the office.
3. He drives an expensive car.
4. He had terrible pains in his chest.
5. For dinner, he has to eat fish or chicken.
6. He has to walk one mile before breakfast.
7. Len got his orders from the doctor.
8. He has to exercise at a health club.

D. Comprehension Questions   Listen and circle the correct answer.

1. How old is Len?
2. What happened to him?
3. Where did he have the heart attack?
4. How long was he in the hospital?
5. What does he like to eat?
6. When does he exercise?
7. How many hours a day can he work now?

Structure and Pronunciation (Page 70)

A. Has to, Can, Can't   Listen to these sentences. Write the complete verb you hear. Listen for *has to, can,* or *can't.*

Examples: A: He has to watch his diet.

B: He can eat chicken and fish.

C: He can't eat steak.

1. He has to lose weight.
2. He can't drink regular coffee.
3. He has to drink decaf coffee.
4. He has to exercise before and after work.
5. He can't smoke anymore.
6. He has to slow down at the office.
7. He can't work ten hours a day anymore.

B. Dictation   Listen and copy the sentences you hear.

1. Len has to exercise every day.
2. He can't put salt on his food.
3. Len can't work at night anymore.
4. Len has to walk one mile every morning.
5. Len has to take care of himself.

C. Can or Can't   Listen to these sentences. Complete with *can* or *can't.*

Pronunciation Note: *can* and *can't*

Can is pronounced can. The main verb is stressed

He can walk one mile a day.

Can't is pronounced can't. We often don't hear the t.

Both can't and the main verb are stressed.

He can't put salt on his food.

---

1. I can't eat dairy products.
2. I can eat anything I want.
3. I can't lose weight.
4. I can't relax.
5. I can do 25 pushups.

Listening 2 (Page 71)

Conversations

Conversation 1:

> **Doctor:** How many hours a day are you working now?
> **Len:** Four hours.
> **Doctor:** And how do you feel? Tired?
> **Len:** No, not at all. I'm ready to put in a full day.
> **Doctor:** Try five hours this month. See how you feel.

Conversation 2:

> **Len:** Doctor, I need to talk to you about coffee.
> **Doctor:** Coffee?
> **Len:** I hate decaf coffee. Decaf coffee is hot brown water.
> **Doctor:** Len, you used to drink six or seven cups of coffee a day.
> **Len:** You don't understand. I need a real cup of coffee.
> **Doctor:** OK, have one cup of regular coffee in the morning. But after that one cup, it's all decaf or nothing.

Conversation 3:

> **Doctor:** Your weight is down again. You lost five more pounds.
> **Len:** Yeah, that's 15 pounds altogether.
> **Doctor:** How far are you walking in the morning?
> **Len:** One mile. That takes me about 15 minutes.
> **Doctor:** Good. You can increase that little by little to two miles.

Conversation 4:

> **Doctor:** Are you smoking again?
> **Len:** Well, only five or six a day.
> **Doctor:** Len, smoking is the number one factor in heart problems. You have to stop. Completely. You can't even have one cigarette a day.
> **Len:** I'll try.
> **Doctor:** Len, you were lucky this time.

Conversation 5:

> **Doctor:** Your cholesterol level was 290. Now, it's 270. You need to bring that down to between 200 and 220.
> **Len:** I'm trying.
> **Doctor:** Here's some information on which foods you can eat and which foods to stay away from.
> **Len:** Everything I like is no good for me.
> **Doctor:** Well, Len, it's your heart.
> **Len:** OK, OK. I hear you.

Conversation 6:

> **Doctor:** Len, your blood pressure is still too high.
> **Len:** What is it?
> **Doctor:** 150 over 90. I'm prescribing Dinatol. Take one tablet twice a day, in the morning and in the evening.
> **Len:** OK.

C. Listen and Complete   Listen to the doctor's orders and complete the sentences. When should you take the medication?

1. Take this twice a day.
2. Take one tablet before each meal.
3. Take one tablet every four hours as needed for pain.
4. Take three tablets now, then one tablet three times a day.
5. Take one tablet one hour after each meal.

Speaking (Page 72)

A. Listen and Answer   Listen to the conversation between a patient and doctor who is prescribing some medication. Answer the questions.

D: Here's a prescription for a new medication.
P: How will this help me?
D: Your blood pressure is high. It will lower your blood pressure.
P: How long will I need to take it?
D: I want you to take it for one month, then, we'll check your blood pressure again.
P: How often should I take it?
D: Take two tablets a day, one in the morning and one before you go to sleep.
P: What are the side effects?
D: Sometimes, patients develop headaches. If that happens, call me.
P: Will my insurance cover this medication?
D: You need to speak with your pharmacist. Most prescription plans cover this medication.
P: Can I take a generic brand of this medication?
D: No, this is a new medication.

UNIT 13: Fast Thinking

Listening 1 (Page 75)

Story

Last month, Jim and Sally Wilson went to the park with their children. Jim and Sally sat under the trees and talked and read. The boys played ball. Sally decided to take a picture of the children. She took out her camera and walked over to them. She focused her camera. Then, she heard a woman scream for help. Sally looked up. A man was stealing a woman's purse. He was running in her direction.

Sally thought fast. She took three pictures of the man. When the police came, she gave them the camera.

The next day, one of Sally's photographs was in the newspaper. Under the picture was the story of the robbery. In a few hours, the police knew the man's name and address. They went to his house and arrested him. The man is now serving three months in jail.

C. Match   Listen and write the letter of the correct picture.

1. One of Sally's photographs was in the newspaper.
2. Sally heard a woman scream.
3. Sally took a picture of the man.
4. When the police came, Sally gave them her camera.
5. Jim and Sally sat under the trees and talked and read.
6. A man was stealing a woman's purse.
7. The children played ball.
8. The man is now serving three months in jail.
9. The police arrested the man.

D. Listen and Decide   You will hear a sentence from the story. Decide what happened next. Circle the correct answer.

1. Sally and Jim sat under a tree.
2. Sally decided to take a picture of the children.
3. She heard a scream.
4. A man was running in her direction.
5. The police came.
6. The police learned the man's name and address.
7. The police went to the man's house.

Structure and Pronunciation (Page 76)

B. Dictation   Listen and copy the sentences you hear.

1. A family went to the park.
2. A man stole a woman's purse.
3. A woman took three pictures of the man.
4. She gave the police her camera.
5. The police went to the man's house.
6. They arrested him and put him in jail.

C. Tense Contrast   Listen to these sentences. Decide the tense of the verb. Circle *present*, *past*, or *future*.

1. He goes to the park on Sunday.
2. He takes a lot of pictures of his children.
3. His wife gave him a new camera.
4. The camera takes great pictures.
5. He's going to take pictures at his son's soccer game.
6. He sent some photographs to his mother.
7. His mother likes to get pictures of her grandchildren.
8. He's going to put the photos in an album.
9. He's going to buy a telephoto lens.
10. He went to the camera store.

Listening 2 (Page 77)

Conversations

Conversation 1:

A: I can't believe it!
B: John was such a nice person.
A: Yeah. He always said, "Good morning."
B: But why? Why did he do it?
A: Who knows?

Conversation 2:

A: You're not serious!
B: I am. John robbed a woman in the park.
A: You're kidding! Are they sure it was John?
B: They're sure. Some woman took his picture. Look here. His picture is on the front page.
A: That's John all right! Whoa!

Conversation 3:

A: Did you see this?
B: No.
A: Here, look at this picture.
B: That's John! What did he do?
A: He stole some woman's purse.
B: Really?
A: Yes, really. Read the story.

Conversation 4:

A: You're not going to believe this.
B: What?
A: The police were here about an hour ago.
B: Here? At our apartment building?
A: They arrested John.
B: John List? The man who lives upstairs?
A: Yeah. They said he robbed a woman in the park yesterday.
B: Stop!
A: It's true. They took him away in a police car.

C. Statement or Question

Listen to each sentence about the story. If it is a statement, put a period at the end of the sentence. If it shows surprise, put a question mark at the end.

Examples: STATEMENT: John robbed a woman.

　　　　　 QUESTION: John robbed a woman?

1. John robbed a woman?
2. His picture is in the newspaper.
3. He stole her purse?
4. John's a nice guy.
5. Some woman took his picture.
6. The police came here.
7. They were here?
8. They arrested him?
9. They arrested him today.
10. He's in jail?

Speaking (Page 78)

B. Listen and Retell

Listen to two students talk about a robbery. Retell the story in your own words.

A: Were you ever robbed?
B: Yes, right here at school.
A: Here? When?
B: Just last month.
A: What happened?
B: I was in the elevator and it was packed. There were lots of people on the elevator, all crowded together. I had my purse on my shoulder, but it was open at the top. When I got to class, I went into my purse to get a pen, and I saw that my wallet was gone.
A: Did you go to security?
B: Yes, I told them what happened. Later, in the afternoon, they called me. A custodian found my wallet in the basket in the ladies room. Someone took the money, it wasn't much, but all my documents and my credit card were still in the wallet.
A: You're lucky. The documents are more important than the money.

UNIT 14: The Accident

Listening 1 (Page 80)
Story

Last night, Kim was driving home from work. She was on Broad Street. Traffic was heavy and she was driving carefully. At the intersection of Broad Street and Park Avenue,

Kim had the green light and drove into the intersection. Suddenly, a sports car went through the red light and crashed into the side of Kim's car. No one was hurt, but the damage to Kim's car was heavy. She couldn't drive home.

The police arrived in five minutes. Kim explained the accident. She said she had the green light and the other driver went past the red light. Then, the officer spoke to the other driver. Kim couldn't believe his story! He told the officer that the accident was Kim's fault. He said that Kim passed the red light! The officer looked around and asked, "Did anyone see the accident? Were there any witnesses?" A man was standing on the sidewalk. He walked over to the officer and said, "I was driving right in back of this woman. Her story is correct. That man went through the red light and hit the side of her car."

Structure and Pronunciation (Page 82)

B. Dictation

Listen and copy the sentences you hear.

1. Kim had an accident on her way home from work.
2. Another car hit her car.
3. No one was hurt.
4. Did anyone see the accident?
5. A witness spoke to the police officer.

C. Listen for Stress

Underline the stressed word in each sentence.

1. <u>Her</u> story is correct.
2. <u>This</u> man passed the red light.
3. She had the <u>green</u> light.
4. He had the <u>red</u> light.
5. <u>I</u> had the green light.
6. <u>You</u> had the red light.
7. He said the accident was <u>Kim's</u> fault.
8. Kim was driving <u>carefully</u>.
9. The other driver <u>lied</u>.
10. The accident was <u>his</u> fault.

Listening 2 (Page 83)
Conversations

Conversation 1:

Officer: OK, let me get the facts.
Driver: Well, I was driving along First Street.
Officer: OK, you were driving along First Street.
Driver: And that woman just backed out of her driveway, right into the street. She didn't stop at the end of her driveway and check to see if anyone was coming.
Officer: She didn't stop and check?
Driver: No, she just came right into the street. And I hit her.

Conversation 2:

> Officer: OK, let me hear your story.
> Driver: Well, I was backing out of my driveway. And I stopped at the end to see if anyone was coming.
> Officer: You stopped at the end of your driveway?
> Driver: Yes. I always stop at the end. And I didn't see anyone.
> Officer: You didn't see anyone?
> Driver: No. And I backed into the street and this man hit me.

Conversation 3:

> Officer: I'm filling out the police report. So, you were driving along Bay Avenue.
> Driver: Yes. I was driving along Bay, in back of that minivan. And suddenly, he stopped real fast. I couldn't stop in time. It was hard to see him because he didn't have any taillights.
> Officer: He didn't have any taillights?
> Driver: No, he didn't.
> Officer: OK. Let me check on that.

Conversation 4:

> Officer: I need some information for the accident report.
> Driver: Well I was driving along Bay Avenue, and a dog ran out in front of my car.
> Officer: A dog ran out in front of your car.
> Driver: I had to stop real fast, so I jammed on my brakes. And the car in back of me hit me, really hard.

C. Repeating or Questioning You will hear eight short conversations between a driver and a police officer. Listen to the examples, then, circle *repeating* or *questioning*.

In the first example, the officer is repeating the information.

> Driver: I was driving along First Street.
> Officer: You were driving along First Street.

In the second example, the officer is questioning the information. The intonation is the same as for a question.

> Driver: I was driving along First Street.
> Officer: You were driving along First Street?

1. **A:** I was driving along First Street.
   B: You were driving along First Street.
2. **A:** She didn't stop at the end of the driveway.
   B: She didn't stop at the end of the driveway?
3. **A:** I was backing out of my driveway.
   B: You were backing out of your driveway.
4. **A:** I stopped at the end of the driveway.
   B: You stopped at the end of your driveway?
5. **A:** I didn't see him coming.
   B: You didn't see him coming?
6. **A:** A dog ran in front of my car.
   B: A dog ran in front of your car.
7. **A:** He didn't have any taillights.
   B: He didn't have any taillights?
8. **A:** I don't want to go to the hospital.
   B: You don't want to go to the hospital?

Speaking (Page 84)

B. Listen and Answer Read the questions below, then, listen to two students talk about an accident. Circle the questions you can answer. Listen again and answer the questions.

1: Oh, my gosh. Amy! Look at you!
2: I was in an accident.
1: What happened?
2: I was driving along Central Avenue. It was about 9:00 in the morning, very little traffic. And suddenly, this other car went right past the stop sign and hit me.
1: Were you in the car alone?
2: Yes, thank goodness. The kids were at school.
1: What about the other driver?
2: She was hurt, pretty badly hurt She was talking on her cell phone, not paying attention. She's going to be okay, but she has a lot of cuts and a broken leg. She was in the hospital for about five days.
1: When did this happen?
2: About a week ago. Last Tuesday.
1: How's your car?
2: It's completely totaled. I'm going to need a new car.
1: Well, I'm sorry to hear about all this. Let me know if I can drive you anywhere.
2: Thanks.

UNIT 15: My Neighbor

Listening 1 (Page 87)
Story

One morning I was walking down Fourth Street. I was going to visit a friend. As I was walking on a quiet street, two men jumped out and mugged me. They took my coat and my money. They beat me, then, they left me in an alley.

A short time later, a man passed by the alley. He was from my neighborhood. I shouted, "Help me." I knew he was going to help me. He said, "I'll get the police." Then, he left. I waited, but he never came back.

A few hours later, a second man passed the alley. I called, "Please help me." I knew he was going to help me because we went to the same church. But he acted like he didn't see me. He turned and left.

It was getting late. I knew I needed help. It was almost dark when a third man passed the alley. I didn't know him. He dressed differently. He wasn't from my country. I didn't think he was going to help me. But he saw me and felt sorry for me. He stopped and called the police. He stayed with me and waited for the ambulance.

The next day, the doctor said to me, "It's a good thing that man stopped and helped you. You almost died. Who was he, a neighbor?"

I thought for a minute, then said, "Yes, he was."

C. Listen and Write the letter
Listen to the sentences and write the letter of the correct picture.

1. He stopped and called the police.
2. He dressed differently.
3. Two men jumped out and mugged me.
4. The next day, the doctor talked to me.
5. They left me in an alley.
6. I was walking down Fourth Street.
7. A man from my neighborhood passed the alley.
8. He stayed with me and waited for the ambulance.
9. He acted like he didn't see me.

E. Comprehension Questions
Listen and circle the correct answer.

1. Where was this man going?
2. When did the men mug him?
3. What did they take?
4. Where did they leave him?
5. How long was he there?
6. Who was the real neighbor?

Structure and Pronunciation (Page 88)

A. Past Tense You will hear two verbs. If they are the same, circle *same*. If they are different, circle *different*.

1. call   called
2. jumped   jumped
3. walk   walked
4. turned   turned
5. act   acted
6. help   helped
7. stayed   stayed
8. arrived   arrived
9. ask   asked
10. die   died

B. -ed Endings Listen to the pronunciation of these verbs. Write the number of syllables you hear. Then, practice saying the past tense of these verbs with a partner.

1. waited   6. died
2. called   7. passed
3. stopped   8. helped
4. acted   9. shouted
5. stayed   10. dressed

C. Dictation Listen and copy the sentences you hear.

1. Two men mugged me.
2. The first man never came back.
3. The second man turned and left.
4. The third man stopped and called the police.
5. He stayed with me and waited for the ambulance.
6. It's a good thing that man helped you.

Listening 2 (Page 89)

Conversations

Conversation 1:

Dispatcher: Springfield Police.
Man: My car is gone! Somebody stole my car!
Dispatcher: Your address?
Man: I'm at work. Wells Industries, 357 Second Street. I parked my car in the parking lot in back of the building this morning. Now, it's not there.
Dispatcher: We'll send someone right over.

Conversation 2:

Dispatcher: Springfield Police.
Woman: Please! Hurry! There's a woman on the street, she's screaming.
Dispatcher: Give me the address.
Woman: Weston Street. 32 Weston Street.
Dispatcher: Stay on the line. Can you see her?
Woman: Yes. A man is pushing her into a car. She's trying to get away from him.

Conversation 3:

Dispatcher: Springfield Police.
Man: There's someone breaking into my neighbor's house. A man just broke the window and climbed in!
Dispatcher: What's your address?
Man: 126 Maple Avenue. It's the house on the left of me.
Dispatcher: Don't hang up. I'm sending a patrol car. You can help us. Which window did he climb in? Can you see the window . . . .

Conversation 4:

Dispatcher: Springfield Police.
Woman: Something's going on in the apartment downstairs.
Dispatcher: Where do you live?
Woman: 462 Salem. In the Salem Apartments. Apartment 4B.
Dispatcher: What's happening?
Woman: Two men are fighting. They're real angry. They're shouting and calling each other names.
Dispatcher: We're sending someone over immediately.

B. Same or different Read each sentence. Then, listen to the sentence. Decide if the meaning of the two sentences is the same or different. Circle *same* or *different*.

1. My car is gone!
2. Hurry!
3. Don't hang up.
4. She's trying to get away.
5. Someone is breaking into my neighbor's house.
6. They are shouting and calling each other names.
7. There's something going on in the apartment downstairs.

Speaking (Page 90)

A. The Robbery You are a clerk in a jewelry store. A few minutes ago a woman came into the store and asked to look at some expensive necklaces. Suddenly, she pulled out a gun, took the jewelry, and asked for the money in the cash register. Now, a police officer is asking you questions. Circle the correct answer.

1. What did she take?
2. How long was she in the store?
3. Was anyone else in the store?
4. What did she look like?
5. What was she wearing?
6. Did she have a gun?
7. What did she say?
8. Do you remember anything special about her?
9. Which way did she go when she left the store?

INDEX

PHOTO CREDITS

Collins COBUILD Dictionaries transform the learner's dictionary into the ultimate resource for English language learners.

- Full Sentence Definitions
- Word Webs
- Word Links
- Word Partnerships
- Interactive CD-ROM

Do you have yours?

Collins COBUILD Intermediate Dictionary of American English
Softcover with CD-ROM 978-1-4240-0776-9

Collins COBUILD Advanced Dictionary of American English
Softcover with CD-ROM 978-1-4240-0363-1

CPSIA information can be obtained
at www.ICGtesting.com
Printed in the USA
FFHW01n1349200918
48508811-52369FF